WALKING WITH TIGERS

JOHN BLACK

© 2018 by John Black
All rights reserved. No part of this book may be reproduced, stored in a retrieval system or transmitted in any form or by any means without the prior written permission of the publishers, except by a reviewer who may quote brief passages in a review to be printed in a newspaper, magazine or journal.

The final approval for this literary material is granted by the author.

First printing

This is a true story. All names, dates and facts are correct.

ISBN: 978-1-61296-992-3
PUBLISHED BY BLACK ROSE WRITING
www.blackrosewriting.com

Printed in the United States of America
Suggested Retail Price (SRP) $18.95

Walking with Tigers is printed in Minion Pro

This book is dedicated to our Dads, Perry and Gib.
Two great guys, who left us too soon.

ACKNOWLEDGMENTS

When I was a junior at Lewiston High School in Lewiston, Idaho I enrolled in a Journalism class taught by Mr. Holbrook who was an old-school taskmaster who preached the five W's of journalism and worked his students like we were cadets in boot camp. He made us learn and, because of him, I became a journalist of sorts and wrote part-time to help with college costs. I never knew Mr. Holbrook's first name and was about to look it up for the purposes of this note when it suddenly struck me – why? MISTER Holbrook is just fine, thank you!

I always talked about writing a book one day but it was just that – talk. Two careers, a family, love of golf and fishing and plain old procrastination kept it from happening.

Then, two remarkable young men whom I had known since they were kids, started a rare adventure and I thought "maybe I should get off my tired butt and tell their story." So, I talked to Joel and Geno and we decided to give it a go.

Special thanks to Joel, the book's co-hero. He was open, honest and getting to know him was an honor. Holly, what can I say? You were always there to talk and give encouragement. You made me laugh and brightened the day. Lona, Bob, Jim, JoAnne, Susan, Dick, Barbara, Ed, Rob, and Nick – thanks so much! There is no way this happens without your willingness to give time and insights.

To life-long friend Tom Thorpe, thanks for the advice and pointing me in the right direction. Reagan Rothe, you are awesome. Agreeing to take on a book with no ending was very cool on your part.

Then there is Geno, the other co-hero. There is no way to thank you enough. Writing e-mails at midnight, calling between flights when you were dog tired, and giving up a little Holly and Hudson time made the story come alive. There is no way this project comes together without you. You're the greatest!

Finally, the very best of all! My wife, nurse, partner, editor, Microsoft word consultant and all around good gal, Marilyn! So many thanks to give you but maybe most of all, thanks for keeping me from throwing the laptop against the wall when it misbehaved! Love you!

WALKING WITH TIGERS

PROLOGUE

SUNDAY, AUGUST 16TH, 2016
PUMPKIN RIDGE GOLF CLUB
NEAR PORTLAND, OREGON
6:10 PM

The mission was clear for Jack Maguire as he walked to the 18th tee on the iconic Pumpkin Ridge Golf Course. If he made birdie, he would make enough money at the WinCo Foods Portland Open to earn his PGA card and become eligible to enter the tour's tournaments in 2017.

However, if the former Florida State University star made par or worse, he would fall short and could only get into tour events through other, more difficult qualifying methods.

The pressure was intense and the Golf Channel's live coverage made it possible for viewers to share the drama. Maguire had put himself into this precarious position by missing very makeable birdie putts on the three previous holes. Now he had absolutely no margin for error.

But there was a good chance he would succeed. Pumpkin's 18th, the tournament's 72nd and final hole, is a reachable par five and several players in the field had successfully hit the green in two shots. Maguire had both the experience under pressure and the firepower to do it.

He did not get the ball on the putting surface in two but he did the next best thing by leaving the ball in perfect position for a simple, straight forward pitch shot. Getting the ball in the hole in two more shots seemed likely for a player with Maguire's talent.

The pitch shot seemed perfectly struck but it ran a bit more than planned and ended up some 12 feet from the cup. Suddenly, Maguire's odds of making birdie swung to about 50 – 50. He began to study his putt and, even through the lens of the television camera, you could feel the tension.

***

15 MILES AWAY
A RENTAL HOUSE IN BEAVERTON, OR.

Joel Dahmen and two friends were sitting in a nearby rental house and the tension was every bit as intense as it was on the green at Pumpkin Ridge. At this exact second, Dahmen sat 25th on the money list of the Web.Com Tour. If Maguire missed the putt, he would remain in that position and it would be he, not Maguire who would be getting the coveted PGA card.

For most of the year earning the card seemed a cinch for Dahmen. He got off to a fast and consistent start and was earning a check almost every week. Getting into to the top 25 seemed to be a no-brainer and the attitude of Dahmen and those around him was one of quiet confidence. He was headed to the big time, the Mecca of professional golf. There was no stopping him.

Then suddenly things turned ugly. He missed five cuts in a row and took another week off citing fatigue. He had fallen to 22nd on the money list and it now looked like he had to make the cut in the tour's final event to secure the right to play in the higher paying and more prestigious tour in 2017.

But, it didn't happen. He shot an opening round 73 on Thursday and followed with a demoralizing 74 on Friday. He was suffering on the back nine Friday as the reality of the situation sunk in. As far as he knew, his dream of playing on the big tour was gone.

"I had a really big cry with my girlfriend Lona Skutt right out in the middle of the driving range. I was crying the entire back nine holes as I knew I was missing the cut and felt I had let everyone down," said Dahmen.

Caddie Geno Bonnalie was suffering with Dahmen and sharing his pain. "It was a helpless feeling. I was watching my best friend suffering with every step and there was nothing I could do to help. Finally, I just hugged him and said I love you man and kind of broke down," said Bonnalie.

Geno's wife Holly had flown to Portland the day before the opening round and she immediately felt things were different. "Usually, Joel is calm and relaxed before a tournament but the minute I saw him I knew things were different. He wasn't himself and it was obvious that he was very nervous," she observed.

Joel agreed.

"The slump created a pressure I had never experienced. It was different than anything I had ever felt on the golf course and I didn't handle it. I had rented this big house many weeks previously and had invited friends and family to join me for what was to be a major weekend celebration. Now there would be no victory lap. Friday night was a real downer," Dahmen related.

Skutt went to Geno Friday evening because she knew he was adept in analyzing odds and assessing probabilities. "Straight up, what are his chances now?" she asked. "Sadly only about 2%. Too many things have to fall just right," Bonnalie predicted.

But, things brightened a bit on Saturday morning. A supportive text from Joel's father Ed pointed out that he still had a chance if the right sequence of events happened during the weekend. Then, Joel's chances got even more realistic when he learned players 23 – 28 on the money list had also missed the cut.

By Sunday evening it all came down to the 18th hole and competitor Jack Maguire.

***

THE HOME OF JIM AND JOANNE BONNALIE
LEWISTON, IDAHO

Geno and Holly made the 350 mile trip from Portland to their home in Lewiston, Idaho on Sunday morning. They arrived when Maguire was on the 14th hole and, at that exact second, they knew the importance of Maguire's situation and its potential effect on their future. With their nerves on full scale alert they went to Geno's parent's house to watch the drama on father Jim's man cave, 70 inch big screen.

"But Geno couldn't watch. He turned his back, sat on Jim's bow flex machine and listened to the audio," said Holly.

"Geno's parents and I watched nervously. We knew what was at stake for Geno and Joel and we had major butterflies. But, Geno? He was in a frenzy," Holly laughed.

Bonnalie has been Dahmen's caddie since 2014 and their relationship is special according to both men. They grew up playing golf together and have been friends since boyhood.

They had grown even closer on the tournament trail and its ups and downs. For the past two years they had survived on a meager budget, rushed from town to town, and in the words of the old Wide World of Sports, had seen the thrill of victory and the agony of defeat.

They had worked hard on and off the course and went through countless ordeals, periods of loneliness, thoughts of self-doubt and all the other emotions and experiences that had put them on the road to getting the coveted PGA card.

Now, their fate rested in the hands of someone else.

***

PUMPKIN RIDGE 18TH HOLE
BEAVERTON RENTAL HOUSE, BONNALIE HOME IN LEWISTON
6:30 pm

Maguire strikes his putt…

Jim Bonnalie says "he missed it left!"…

Dahmen watches the putt roll past the cup and bows his head in relief…

Geno Bonnalie turns around and tapped by his mother, screams, screams and screams some more…

Geno phones Joel and there is more screaming, yelling and distant high fives…

"We've made it! We're on the PGA Tour," Geno yells.

And, indeed they were! Their joint dream had come true. They had earned the right to go head-to-head with the best golfers on the planet.

They were about to go walking with Tigers.

PART ONE

CHAPTER ONE
JOEL

One doesn't have to be around Joel Dahmen too long before realizing he is a bright and determined young man.

His early years were right out of a Leave it to Beaver script, complete with loving and supportive parents, comfortable living conditions and a boat load of friends. He was the second child born to Ed and Jolyn Dahmen in Lewiston, Idaho in 1987. Brother Zach was two years older. In 1996, the family moved to a nice home across the river in Clarkston, Washington.

His grandfather Dick Riggs is a community icon. He is a noted educator who was a school superintendent and teacher for over 40 years. He is also a historian and author of five books including MEMORIES OF JOLYN, a tribute to his daughter and Joel's mother. Nearly everyone in the small community knows and respects him.

"We had a great life. My dad worked long hours to make sure we had everything we needed and our childhood was filled with nothing but love and great family memories," Dahmen reflected.

Mother Jolyn was a high school basketball player who also fulfilled her life-long dream of being a Vandal by playing ball at the University of Idaho. It became apparent at a young age that Joel had inherited her talent and love for sport. He played in all the youth sports leagues and was one of those kids who excelled at whatever he tried.

Ed introduced him to golf and, by age six, he was able to play along with his dad's group at Bryden Canyon municipal golf course in Lewiston. "The rule was simple. I could play as long as I kept up. If I fell behind, I had to pick up. I learned quickly." Dahmen said.

Ed tells a story about Joel before he started playing on the golf course.

"The Bryden Canyon owner/operators held a youth golf camp and, even though Joel was only four and a half, they let him in the seven and under group because his attention span was so good. At the end of the camp a putt, chip and drive competition was held and they allowed Joel to enter these also. In the long-drive segment, all the older bigger kids had hit their drives and little Joel stepped up as the last entrant. Those who were measuring moved toward the little guy so they could measure his drive and were left agape when Joel sailed he ball way over their heads and up the fairway. It was very funny to watch their expressions," Ed beamed.

***

Young Joel was a normal kid who loved every kind of bat, ball or club he could find. He lived for sports. Brother Zach was totally different and was more interested in the arts.

"Joel had a way with words even as a very young kid. He would talk about anything and seemed just as comfortable talking to adults about adult things as he was talking to other kids about sports and stuff," grandmother Barbara Riggs recalled. "He was always easy to be around and liked all people," she added.

Ed Dahmen agreed and shared a poem Joel wrote to his mom when he was five. Ed still has it in a scrapbook.

I like the way you look
I like the way you cook
I guess I meant to say
Happy Mother's Day!

***

Young Joel's golf development was so quick that at age nine he was encouraged to join the heralded Washington State Golf Association's junior program, a group that runs competitive golf tournament for youngsters in several age groups.

He showed his ability to compete right away winning or finishing near the top in almost every tournament he entered. In fact, he won his first of many state championships at age 10 competing in the 11 and under age group. He was beginning to make a real name for himself on the local golf scene.

***

"Pay the kids!"

Joel was 12 when 15-year-old Geno Bonnalie called and asked him to be his partner at a tournament in Grangeville, Idaho, a small town about 70 miles from Lewiston. Joel was excited as could be. This would be his first non-Junior tournament and this cool older kid from Lewiston wanted him as a partner. The tournament was a two-day event and they would be staying overnight. All of this was a bit much for Ed Dahmen and he was inclined to say no.

Then Jim Bonnalie, Geno's dad, introduced himself to Ed and Jolyn and "I knew everything would be fine," Ed said. "We could instantly see that the Bonnalie's were fine people and, even though Joel and Geno would be staying in their own room, we weren't worried because Jim was going to be there too. Plus, Joel was practically begging to go and I didn't have the heart to say no."

The boys were the only young people in the entire field. They did very well in Saturday's round and right after they finished, Ed got a call from a very excited Joel. "Dad, they have this horse race thing and Geno and I can win a whole bunch of money. Can I bet on myself, dad?" Ed wasn't sure this was a good idea but said okay reminding Joel that he would be risking his own money.

The Horse Race field was a bunch of men who played early in the day and, for many it was a beer drinking event as well as a best ball golf game. Basically, every team member put in ten dollars and the lowest score on a hole won the pot. If one tied, all tied and the players moved on to the next hole where ten more dollars was added to the pot.

The first two holes were tied but Joel won the third with a birdie. A vocal participant then bellowed "pay the kids!" This became the tournament chant because Geno eagled the fifth and sixth holes and closed things out with yet another birdie on the ninth. "The kids" went on to dominate the tournament and won multiple prizes.

"Joel came home with this wad of cash and he was absolutely glowing. I guess this was his first experience of golf for money," Ed Dahmen joked.

Grangeville marked the first of many winning experiences for Geno and Joel and a kind of big brother/young brother bond was formed that is still very much in place today. Joel was a boy but had a man's golf game and Geno's encouragement and insight helped him take his game to the next level. The relationship was perfect for both of them.

***

Joel Dahmen's junior record was impressive and the wins piled up. Then he stunned the area's golf community by winning the Washington State High School tournament as a freshman! The awards and championships kept coming. He won everything in sight and, often as defending champion, went out and won the tournament again the following the next year. The news articles about his junior victories fill four scrapbooks and his trophies liberally grace the Dahmen and Riggs residences.

His dominance of the Northwest junior scene didn't stop there. He won a number of prestigious Lewis-Clark Valley events including the long-standing Lewiston Whing Ding and Sole Survivor multiple times. The combination of these successes was beginning to create a lot of buzz from the locals and he was developing a sizeable following in his home town.

This run of excellence also resulted in an offer of a full ride scholarship to the University of Washington which was readily accepted. At age 17 Joel was on top of the world. His potential upside seemed unlimited and locally, he was a true celebrity. Things were as bright as they could be.

Then tragically, things changed.

***

Mother Jolyn was diagnosed with pancreatic cancer in October of 2004 and six months later she passed away at age 46. Joel was very close to his mother and her sickness hurt him more deeply than words can describe. It was a terrible time for him and he missed her with all of his heart.

Jolyn had a tremendous zest for life and many friends commented that they loved her laugh which always cheered up everyone around her. She laughed hard and often and seemed to always have a friendly smile on her face.

She had been her high school's valedictorian, representative to Girls State and a cheerleader. She had graduated from the University of Idaho with honors and became a dearly loved and respected teacher. Her students, fellow faculty members and parents adored her. Soon after her passing one of her students wrote the following:

MRS. DAHMEN
BY MICHAELLE BRAWNER
6TH GRADE WHITMAN SCHOOL

I really don't know what to say,
Except I'll love Mrs. Dahmen after this day,
She was the best woman I have ever known,
And now she has finally flown
To a place where she can rest
And do what she was meant to do best,
I loved her so much, you can't believe
I know a lot of people who knew her
And who were close to her will grieve,
I don't know how long, no one can tell,
All we can think of is that she is well

It is almost impossible to capture how many people Jolyn had touched during her short time on earth but the following beautiful excerpt from her dad in the book *MEMORIES OF JOLYN* speaks volumes:

2005 Call of Death
By Dick Riggs

April 18, 2005 was the saddest day of my life. Our beloved daughter, Jolyn Riggs Dahmen died at 1:05 pm that day at her Clarkston home. Barbara and I had been with her all morning, but we had been home a couple of hours when her husband Ed called us and said she had passed away. Jolyn had been told six months before her death that she had pancreatic cancer and had only a few months to live. Even though we knew we thought our prayers would be answered and she wouldn't die. I have the thought from time to time since Sissy (our family name for her) died whether it's easier to lose a loved one who lingers and dies slowly or to lose one suddenly (accident). I suppose there is no real answer. Like our parents, our children are precious and mean everything to us. Our Jolyn was an all-American daughter to us, beautiful on the outside and inside, a friend to many (over 400 sympathy cards and a big church funeral). She was high school valedictorian and most valuable player in basketball and she graduated from the University of Idaho with high academic honors and was president of her sorority. She wanted to be an Idaho Vandal since we took her there to see football games when she was a junior high student. Much to my satisfaction she became a teacher and taught kindergarten at Whitman School in Lewiston.

Jolyn was 46 when she passed away and she left behind her husband Ed, her sons Zach and Joel (19 and 17), her brothers Doug and Matt and her grandpa and grandma Riggs who felt very guilty because they were still alive and she wasn't. All of us who knew her miss her, but I think of our four grandchildren who really never got to know her. They are 15, 12, 10 and 9 as I write this in December of 2014, and I think they would so have enjoyed their Auntie Jo and she would have had such fun with them. I keep a diary journal and since Jolyn's passing, I have "written it as a letter to her each day. I start it out with "Hi, Sissy," or "Dear Precious" and tell her about her boys, our family, her friends, her Vandals, whatever else is going on in my life.

***

Joel was close to his mother who had been with him for most of his golfing successes and school functions. One special family tradition was prom dinner night. The first one was held for Zach and his first prom date and it soon became so popular Joel, a couple of his friends and their dates begged for their turn.

Basically, it went like this. Ed would dress like a high class maître d' and be the waiter for the evening, complete with towel over the arm the appropriate "right away sir" and formal in every way five star service. Jolyn would prepare an elaborate dinner and the couples would sit down to the town's finest dining right in the Dahmen living room. The kids loved it!

Two months after Jolyn passed, Grandpa Dick and Grandma Barbara carried on the tradition in first-class fashion at the Riggs' residence. It was an unbelievable act of grandparental love and deep respect but it wasn't the same. Nobody could ever be a substitute for Jolyn.

***

Dealing with the long, terrible illness and watching his mom die a slow death was more than just difficult for Joel and, as one might expect, it put him in a major mental tailspin. The problem was accelerated because, though Joel had been a great communicator, he refused to talk about his mother's situation. He went into a shell and saw his mother die day-by-day and refused to grieve properly or openly share his feelings.

This still bothers Ed. "I look back and feel very bad. I didn't do enough or pay enough attention to my boys. I was so focused on prayers and hoping the Lord would spare Jolyn that I wasn't thinking as much about them as much as I should have been. Sure, I was hurting big time but so were they and I should have insisted on grief counseling or something to help them cope better. I regret the way I responded as a dad."

So, Joel was still dealing with this in a major way when he went to Seattle to claim his University of Washington scholarship. Things didn't work out. "Golf wise I was okay but I lacked life focus and maturity and just quit going to class. Things were too far gone. I was a small town kid without a lot of drive or direction to do anything. I missed my mother and didn't handle that well at all. I plain flunked out," Joel remembered.

With no other options on the table and a bitter taste in his mouth regarding college, Dahmen moved to Scottsdale, Arizona and declared that he was now a professional golfer. He bounced around the mini tours, played in local Gateway events and tried to advance his position in the golf world. Things were moving slowly in that regard and he was having very little success. "I wasn't getting any better. I was with a bunch of other golf wannabees and we spent a lot of time partying and exercising practically no discipline. We were more about having a good time than getting better at golf. Our work ethic sucked," Dahmen admitted.

In 2010 Joel had moved in with two golfing companions from his high school days who were now attending Arizona State University. Trevor Arnone graduated from ASU and later returned to the Lewis-Clark Valley and became a successful investment advisor. Kyle Rogers now works for Amazon in the Seattle area.

Arnone and Rogers enjoyed a good party as much as anyone but both had jobs and were going to school so they had pretty full schedules. Joel on the other hand did practically nothing. He played in some skin games with other guys from the area and played in mini tour events once in a while, but mostly he sat around and watched television or played video games. "If he did practice, it was late in the day and short in duration," Arnone recalled.

Plus there was to be more cancer in his life. His brother Zach was diagnosed with testicular cancer and successfully treated. Then in 2011, Joel got the same diagnosis.

"I remember when he told us," Arnone said. "We were sitting in the living room and he shared the bad news. We were shocked. Guys our age aren't supposed to worry about things like that."

He had surgery to remove the testicle and underwent chemotherapy treatment that would go on eight hours a day, every day, for several weeks. Dahmen was sick, weak and prone to throwing up.

"At the beginning, it was tough," Dahmen said. "You're not sure where to go or what to do or how healthy you're going to be or what your long-term goal can be. I was saying Why me? I was pouting a lot."

Luckily for Joel, in February of 2012, he had met Lona Skutt, a pretty young graphic artist who was working as a waitress at the time. They hit it off immediately and soon became a couple. It was Lona who provided a badly needed "kick in the butt when I was at my lowest point," shared Joel.

"In the winter of 2013 I was playing lousy golf and getting nowhere. I was broke and depressed. We were pretty much living off of Lona's earnings and I was laying around the house pretty much feeling sorry for myself. One day she got fed up and told me to get off my dead butt and either aggressively go after my golf dream or give it up and get a job! She told me she was sick of being part of my pity party. So, I took my last bit of money and took a golf lesson," Dahmen recalled.

"I went to PGA professional Scott Sackett who was highly recommended and I told him I needed to learn how to change my swing so I could perform better under pressure. He gave me a couple of positive thoughts and three weeks later I won $15,000 on a Gateway event. That was a fortune to us," Joel said fondly.

Skutt's talk also inspired a better work ethic. 'I renewed my respect and outlook on the game and changed my goals. My practice habits and several other things weren't on track with PGA professionals and I rededicated myself and began a more disciplined approach," Dahmen shared.

"Then, I kept it going and played my best golf ever on the Canadian Tour in 2014," he added.

Indeed he did. After floundering in 2013, he got rolling in 2014 and won the Canadian Award of Merit as the Canadian Tour's leading money winner and therefore, got a full exemption to the Web.com Tour for 2015. So, in a very real sense, it was Lona who had gotten Joel off his butt and back in the chase of his dream.

CHAPTER TWO
GENO

Many people go through life content with the status quo, never wanting to rock the boat. Geno Bonnalie is not one of them

Other people have dreams but never take the initiative to make them come true. Geno is not one of those people either.

In the days leading up to Christmas in 2010, Geno decided he wanted to make golf history so he contacted the people at the Guinness Book of World Records to get their guidelines on how to set a recognized record for the most holes played in a week. He also decided to challenge the birdie record for the same time frame. The previous record was 1880 and 310, respectively.

Geno also saw this as a golden opportunity to do something special for his seven-year old cousin, Tina Flerchinger. She had been suffering her entire young life from a rare disease called Cystinosis and Bonnalie decided to combine his quest with a fund-raising effort for research. He got pledges from individuals and was able to donate $15,000 to the cause.

He worked with the staff of the Lewiston Golf and Country Club to set up a course that would meet the Guinness distance requirements and created "Geno tees" for all 18 holes. He recruited dozens of club members who served as combination scorers and witnesses and other people who drove in front of him to alert on course players that "Geno was coming through!"

On June 27, 2011 he teed it up at number one at 4:22am and the race was on! He played 18 rounds (324 holes) on the first day and could barely crawl out-of-bed the next morning. He developed sore muscles, blisters and had to fight 100 degree heat and fatigue but he kept going and going day after day. "The very worst thing was the first shot of each morning. My grip felt like I was grabbing razor blades and I would literally whimper," Bonnalie said.

The feat drew tremendous interest locally and people put signs in their windows. One big one on number 10 read "GO GENO GO" and it became the symbol of the feat. The Lewiston Morning Tribune and KLEW TV kept locals up to date and people yelled encouragement from the street, golf carts, patios, and clubhouse as he rolled around the course at an amazing clip from dawn to dusk.

The other symbol of the feat was the "Geno Mobile". Bonnalie has a very noticeable golf cart that is lime green and topless and one can see it coming from a long distance. Somehow the old cart was able to make it around for most of the holes with either Geno or a volunteer at the wheel. The cart was almost always surrounded by other carts or people on foot who would run ahead and make sure a ball was on the tee and ready to be hit when he arrived. All of this made for a rather colorful spectacle that was exciting and energizing.

Finally, at 7:30 pm on July 3rd, Geno called it quits. He had played an even 2000 holes and had also shattered the previous birdie record by carding 493 of them. "There was another 90 minutes of sunlight and I could have pressed on but I thought 2000 was a pretty cool number and I was so, so tired," he remembered.

Geno's mother JoAnne was extremely proud of her son and his feat but she was glad to see him quit when we did. "He had sores and blisters everywhere including very bad ones under his armpits. Plus, he had to get a shot in his knee in the middle of the week. The physical toll was way too much for most people."

The local country club members shared the excitement of the event but few were surprised because they knew Geno was a determined, bulldog type of guy who wouldn't quit. The birdie record was no shock either. Geno had been a very good player for a long time and, in fact, he owns the club's course record, an eleven under par 61!

***

The day of the record Geno was in a foursome with three of his favorite playing companions Gabe Alexander, Brian King and Jason Speck. All are Lewiston Country Club members who carry near scratch handicaps. Geno shot a solid 33 on the front nine and was feeling good about things but nobody in the group suspected what was about to happen on the back nine.

He birdied number ten and then drove the 320 yard 11th hole and knocked in a six-footer for eagle to go six under par. He hit it to within an inch on the par three 12th and made a long putt on 13 for two more birdies and suddenly he was 8 under through 13. "It started to get a bit quiet after that," Geno quipped. He did birdie 15 but pars on 16 and 17 seemed to stop the rally and he needed an eagle on 18 to shoot 28 and claim the new course record.

"For some reason I wasn't nervous. I had had great rounds before but could never finish the deal. However, on this special day everything felt right and I had a sense of confidence I haven't experienced either before or since," said Geno.

Sure enough, a massive drive and a solid 6 iron left him with a 12 foot putt on the par 5 and he drained it. "We did have a few adult beverages after that," he quipped.

***

Geno was born on March 19, 1984 in Orofino, Idaho which is in the heart of logging country. Father Jim had a thriving logging business at the time and he still builds logging roads for the Potlatch Corporation. The family moved to nearby Lewiston a few years later and Geno graduated from Lewiston High School in 2002. He has an older brother, Ryan and a younger sister Jade.

Jim was a competitive archer and he taught Geno to shoot when he could barely walk. "We would go to a tournament almost every weekend and I won my first trophy when I was four. It was great and my dad was my best friend so it was really special," smiled Geno.

Jim Bonnalie said Geno was a natural archer. "He caught on right away. He was able to focus on the target and block out the distractions around him and that is not easy. He once shot a perfect score in a contest and that is a real rarity for anyone, let alone a young guy," Jim said.

At age 8 Jim introduced Geno to golf and gave him a few old golf clubs. Geno would hit balls all over a nearby field and would do so for hours on end. "Then, one day I hit this shot that flew all the way over the field, over the road and hit a house! I was hooked for life," Bonnalie laughed.

In the summer, Geno's mom would drop him off at Bryden Canyon Golf Course on her way to work and pick him up on her way home at night. He would play golf all day, every day and did odd jobs like picking up range balls to earn lunch and practice range privileges. This was ideal for Geno who loved every minute and the employees at Bryden Canyon welcomed his company. He was liked and respected by people of all ages.

***

The fourth hole at Bryden Canyon Golf Course is a dogleg par four with a lake on the left and out-of-bounds on the right. The right side features a barbed wire fence that separates the golf course from property owned by the Lewiston Airport Authority. One day Geno was walking down the right side of the fairway when he spotted several golf balls that were over the fence and just a little bit out of reach. This presented a challenge young Geno simply could not resist and he decided to scale the fence and claim the prizes on the other side.

Sometimes things just don't work out. Geno's pant leg caught on the fence and he took a head first dive that resulted in two broken arms. He then had to make a mile long walk to get help. Needless to say, that ended his golf season.

***

At age 12, Jim asked Geno to make a decision. He would either take him to the national junior archery tournament or buy him a new set of Taylor made burner golf clubs. He chose the clubs and his love affair with golf blossomed further.

Geno's passion for the game was legendary around his home but his talent never quite measured up to his inner passion and he had an okay but largely unremarkable junior golf career,

Then in September of 2002, he entered the University of Idaho's PGA program where he was struck by a thunder bolt named Holly.

CHAPTER THREE
HOLLY

Holly Jacobson was Senior Prom Queen and voted "most friendly" by her classmates at Post Falls High school in Post Falls, Idaho. Within five minutes of meeting her, one can see why she won those awards. She is no longer a high school kid of course, but she still comes across as a warm and open person whom you have known for years. She is beyond just likeable.

The other immediate impression one gets is she is firmly grounded and mature beyond her years. She not only supported her husband's decision to give up a secure, well-paying job to become a caddie, she is the one who made it possible.

***

On September 16, 2014, Geno sent the following e-mail to Joel Dahmen:

From: Geno Bonnalie <genobonnalie@hotmail.com>
Sent: Tuesday, September 16, 2014 7:31 AM
To: Joel Dahmen
Subject: Web.com & PGA

Hey buddy,

I've had this typed for some time but I was waiting until you OFFICIALLY locked up that #1 spot. First off, I want to tell you how proud of you I am. I've believed since you were a little tike at Clarkston that you were going to make the

Big Time. Not only do I think you're going to make the big time. I truly believe you will be one of the best players in the World.

That being said, I would like to officially apply for the position of "Joel Dahmen's Caddy" for the Web.com *&* PGA TOUR. *I have been thinking about this for a long time, and I don't want to put any pressure on you to hire me, I just want to explain why I would be a good fit for the job and let you decide. I just want what is best for you and I truly believe that you and I would thrive together.*
    First off, I want to tell you that Holly and I are comfortable financially and we would not rely on you winning in order to live. I don't want you to have any additional weight on your shoulders of you thinking you have to perform so I can eat. This is a job and I understand there may be weeks without any revenue.
    Last time we spoke you said something along the lines of "it's not as fun as you think it is..." I don't think you realize how much I love golf, everything about it. It literally consumes my thoughts. I promise you that no one would work harder than I would. I will be at the course earlier than everyone, I will be a charting/documenting machine. I feel like you and I have the type of relationship where this would be a good fit. You are one of my best friends, and I feel like I can express my opinions and concerns to you without having it affect us personally (not that we would have any issues...just saying). I also understand that you need alone time and time to spend with your friends on Tour. I do not plan on spending every waking second with you, but we will definitely have our time to celebrate after successful tournaments.
    You and I also talked about how caddying full time on the web.com *tour may not be a viable option...I think I could make it work. I know Bob is going to caddy in Mexico/South America, but when you return to the U.S., I would like you to consider me being your guy. I already have a plan to get rid of my truck, and buy a Honda Civic and modify it to be my house. I have also looked at the schedule and know that there are some weeks where it is over 1000 miles to the next location. That's okay. That's only 16 hours & $125 in gas...easy. I know there would be a lot of peanut butter and jelly sandwiches in my future, but I have a way of surviving on nothing. I made it through college. If you would prefer that I only attend a couple events, that's fine too. But I think it'd be best for our partnership if I were to be able to learn your game and how you like to practice, and learn the courses as much as I can.*

The hardest part for me will be being away from Hudson. I'm not going to lie, it's going to be tough. Holly's mom has already talked about getting a place in Lewiston and helping out with him if needed. On the plus side, in our off times I would get to spend quite a bit of time at home.

I do have some requirements from you though if you do consider me for this:

I expect you to give it 100% every week

Never give up

Be completely honest with me at all times

Again, I don't want you to feel like you have to hire me. I want you to hire me because you think I will be the best person for the job. If you think someone else will do better and be a better fit...great. As long as you are successful, happy, and come home to play golf with me every once in a while, I will be a happy camper.

Keep me posted because if you do decide to go another route I need to find a new job.

I love you, and I am so proud of you!

WOOOOO!

***

According to Dahmen, "Geno sent me this formal e-mail applying for the job as my caddie and I kind of laughed because we were best friends. I told him no for four months because I didn't want him sacrificing a paycheck and missing time with his wife Holly and Hudson. But, then I talked to Holly and she convinced me it was the right thing to do for their whole family."

She told Dahmen "Look, he believes in you and he wants to be out there with you. He doesn't want to jump on the train when you get on the PGA Tour, he wants to help you get there. Also, I love this man to death and I don't want him looking back when he is 45 years old and saying, if only..."

This pep talk sealed the deal and the Dahmen-Bonnalie duo premiered in the Web.com Tour event in Mexico in March of 2015.

***

When asked the toughest thing about Geno's new profession, Holly responds quickly. "People we barely know question our decision. They say things like Gee, how do you make ends meet? Can you pay your bills? Aren't you lonely? Many of them mean well but their condescending attitude can be grating sometimes."

"Some people just don't get it. They think Geno is acting selfish playing caddie and caring only about himself and his desires. They imply we have a bad marriage and he is a poor father because he travels so much. Nothing could be further from the truth! I have a husband who loves golf and he is totally happy doing what he cares about for a person he cares about." Holly emphasized.

"Plus, when Geno is home he is really home. Hudson and I have his full attention 24/7. He is not like some fathers who might live at home but work long hours and have little time for their families after a long day. This works for us! We couldn't be happier," Holly added.

It also helps that Holly has a job that she loves and provides her with a good income. She is one of four people who run the successful Basalt Winery in Clarkston and her passion for the business is obvious. "We are like a family and the winery is like our child. We do it all from making the wine to marketing, bottling, distributing, running our tasting room, managing a big wine club, you name it. I can't image doing anything else." she smiled.

She also earns enough to make ends meet with enough left over for an occasional trip to hook up with Geno and Joel. In 2016, these included trips to Hawaii and the Bahamas.

Still, there are stretches when Geno is gone for several weeks at a time and she admits it can get lonely. The couple copes with this by texting, sending e-mails and making phone calls. "It's important that we stay connected. If he has a blister I want to know about it. I care what he had for dinner and how his day went. Luckily, he feels the same way and we manage to stay close regardless of the miles between us," said Holly.

The other huge strength is their families. Geno's parents live in the same neighborhood and the Jacobson's, though 100 miles away, are in touch every day in some way. All are extremely supportive and positively involved the couple's adventure. "My mom and dad are involved. My brothers and sister are involved. My brother's whole law firm is involved. The interest and support are out of this world!" Holly smiled.

***

Holly was born on September 29, 1984 in Coeur d'Alene, Idaho to Ron and Susan Jacobsen. She was the second of three children.

Dad Ron was already a successful banker when Holly was born and the family lived on a beautiful four acre lot in nearby Post Falls, Idaho and had a nice lake cabin in Twin Lakes, a few miles away. The family was raised with strict, conservative Catholic values and Holly remembers missing church only one time while growing up.

"It seems a bit odd that we were raised strict but were also encouraged to speak our mind and think for ourselves. Free expression and new ideas were encouraged and still are. We were always happy and secure and we couldn't have asked for a better childhood," She reflected.

"I did have one issue. I was tall and terribly skinny until I went to college. I was so ugly! Then, I gained 35 pounds and grew boobs," Holly laughed.

She loved life at the University of Idaho where she joined and later became President of her Sorority. It was at a Sorority function in her freshman year that she first encountered Geno and it is he who described their first encounter.

"I had never had a real girlfriend and I was beyond awkward. Then I saw this girl and it was like I was hit by a thunderbolt! I wanted to meet her but when I walked over to her I lost my nerve and stupidly mumbled gee, you're tall and walked away. I felt like an idiot."

"The next semester I saw her in a class and our professor gave us a stupid icebreaker exercise. I had one square left to fill and got the nerve to approach her with the question - Do you sing in the shower? Her reply was "I guess you'll have to find out. "

"It bowled me over! I was in love like a puppy. By May, we were a couple," Bonnalie smiled.

And, Holly's take on this. "He was so cute! Here was this big handsome guy who was shy as could be and he seemed overwhelmed to be talking to a girl. I was fascinated."

As a matter of fact, Geno has never completely grown out of his shyness around women. He tells a story on himself that still makes Joel Dahmen laugh. "We were at a pro-am tournament in Columbus, Ohio and Joel's partner for the day was Danica Patrick, the attractive NASCAR driver. She was so nice and fun and I was a bit in awe. Then in mid round, she got me good."

"She was waggling (relaxing her body before a shot) and she looked over her shoulder and said Geno quit admiring my ass," I about died Geno said. "The truth is I actually WAS admiring her ass."

Joel laughed "Geno turned beet red, he stayed that way for the rest of the day."

"Geno is perfect in my eyes. When we met, my life just clicked," Holly says.

Geno marvels at Holly and her attitude. "She is one of a kind. There is no way I can do what I do without her unbelievable outlook on life and happiness. Honestly, I'm about the luckiest guy on the planet," Geno says fondly.

They married in 2007 at Post Falls and son Hudson was born six years later.

***

The following is a word-for-word description of Holly from her mother, Susan Jacobsen. No edit needed.

Holly is the second of our four children (two girls and two boys) and my only child to throw temper tantrums. Around the age of 2, Holly decided this action would get her what she desired in life. Boy, was she mistaken. One day during a tirade she was joined on the floor by her dad who also kicked and screamed at the top of his lungs. She got up off the floor, gave her dad a quizzical look and walked away, never to try that maneuver again.

As a child, Holly always had a smile on her face and was well loved by all her teachers. In second grade this little gal was the watchdog of the special needs children who were integrated into regular classrooms. Pushing their wheelchairs and wiping their noses. Her empathy towards others was apparent at an early age.

Entering middle school her talking speed was ever increasing. The less she wanted you to know, the faster she spoke. "Hey Dad, isitokif-StaceyandIgoto..."

As parents we would ask her to repeat 4 or 5 times in order to get the whole story. Kids have a way of keeping us parents on our toes.

Shortly after starting college, she mentioned to her dad about this guy she was dating and how excited he was over hitting a golf ball 300 yards. Ron thought there was no way in the world, until he played golf with Geno.

Holly is my most intuitive child. She has a way of knowing what you are feeling before you speak. And she can articulate her thoughts in a spot on manner, getting her point across for others understanding. She hides her true feelings behind her smile but occasionally her eyebrows will shoot up and then you'd better watch out.

Recently, at her sister Lauren's wedding, she gave a most eloquent speech on what married life is. I am including it here as you will understand where her heart lies when it comes to her family. Her little guy Hudson has inherited his mother's empathy, as during the speech when her voice broke he walked up and put his arm around her leg.

Yaya, Dr. Dan...you two are officially official, Mr. & Mrs. Bechtold. I am already loving the ring to that. You guys have had a huge month. Trip to Nepal, medical school graduation, new house, and now the pinnacle of it all...getting married. We could not be more excited for you, and to watch your life unfold together.

No wedding is complete without a little advice, namely advice for you, if you aren't YET aware of this, you will soon learn...Lauren has exquisite taste, and she likes FANCY...if she asks you to pick up tomatoes on the way home, you need to go to whole foods and find the most EXPENSIVE tomatoes they have. If the tomatoes don't cost over $1.50 each then you need to quickly get online and have tomatoes shipped in from an organic, sustainable, non gmo, farm in southern California that is owned by two nuns who adopt children from Africa.

Never, EVER, underestimate the power of a new pair of shoes, or handbag. This will become the most powerful weapon in your arsenal. When in doubt, always go with a new purse as the answer. Don't say I didn't tell you.

Lauren is never wrong, and if she is wrong, she will not want to admit it in the midst of an argument...so Dan, I have an idea...think that at the beginning of each year you need to number cards from 1-10, put the cards into a hat, and draw a number. This will be the number of times you are able to "veto" her.

Every time I am around Lauren I can't keep my hands off of her, and just because you are married Dan, that's not going to change. When we are on family vacations, I might even want to share a bed with her, so you will need to learn, and be willing to...move over.

Remember, life isn't always as glamorous and ideal as this moment right now. It is SO much better than this. It is wonderfully imperfect in every way, shape and form. It is having a broken water heater at the same time you have a malfunctioning furnace, it is baby poop all over your diaper bag and up your arm when you are headed into a meeting or a patient's room. It is trying not to laugh out loud as your spouse disciplines children over something they have done that is ACTUALLY comical. It is arguing about the best way to fix your grass that is covered in moss. It is laying in bed laughing hysterically over something your spouse just told you about his childhood that you have never heard. It is playing "rock, paper, scissors" over who has to clean-up the dog vomit in the hallway, and then as you are trying to decide the baby has a blowout of epic proportions.

Every moment forward is better than this when you have your soul-mate, your best friend, your confidant, and your love to walk the journey.

Most of all, I want to share with you guys, how Yaya came alive when she met you. Her heart settled into the most beautiful rhythm of happy. She called me and said "every time Dan leaves, I cry." Remember that type of love you have for each other, that it is always better to walk together than alone, remember to nourish your relationship. Allow others to make fun of you for how often you talk or text, tell each other everything. Go to bed at the same time, don't EVER say a bad word about your spouse to someone else, and most importantly learn how to laugh at all the mishaps that come along. Laughter is so much better than being angry or bitter. Remember you are in this life together. And we will all be loving and supporting you the whole way. Also, feel free to have some babies.

Cheers!

CHAPTER FOUR
LONA

Everyone needs someone to believe in them and, though Joel Dahmen's support is widespread, nobody is more important to him than girlfriend Lona Skutt.

It was Lona who supplied the motivation to get his career back on target with a bit of tough love when a kick in the butt was needed and it is she who is his biggest booster. She has put her own career on hold because Joel wants her to travel with him this year and she wants to be there to support him. Also, she helps Joel focus on golf by handling scheduling, travel arrangements and financial matters. "I know in my gut he is going to make it and maybe I can help a little," Skutt replied.

She made some trips to Web.com tournaments last year and enjoys the travel and adventure. "We live a crazy life with limited stability but it is never boring! Visiting new places is always fun and we recognize how fortunate we are to try this adventure while we are young. Hey, we can always settle down and get real jobs if this doesn't work out," Lona related.

The frequent travel also plays perfectly into another shared interest. Skutt has always been an adventurous seeker of new food that is both healthy and delicious. On the road she and Joel often seek out the best restaurants and make dinner an important part of their day. In some ways, they are living the dream. Being young, seeing new places and living an adventure are exciting things and Joel and Lona are embracing their situation and enjoying life.

***

Lona was born August 13, 1988 in Newport Beach, California to Lara Davis, a single mother. Two years later Lara met Chad Skutt and in 2000 they were married and Chad legally adopted Lona.

The family lived in an area north of Scottsdale. Chad was a sales representative and Lara was a Human Resource Director for major companies. Both were doing very well financially but didn't like living the corporate lifestyle and in 2001, when Lona was 13, they made a bold decision and decided to completely change their position in life. They quit their jobs and took over a family gas station and petting zoo in Summerville, California, a small town near Reno, Nevada.

"I couldn't even find this place on a map. I thought my parents were taking me to the end of the earth and I wasn't happy at all," Lona said. "However, it was in Summerville that I learned my love of art and the outdoors and it turned out to be a great place to grow up,' she added.

Skutt developed a strong work ethic by watching her parents and how they did things. She got a job before she was 14 and ironically it was at a golf course. She worked in outside services cleaning carts and clubs and picking balls on the driving range. "It was cool. I got an hourly wage and tips and the people were friendly. But, I thought golf was the stupidest thing on earth. That's pretty funny in retrospect,'" Lona laughed.

Her parents wanted her to help at the family business but they didn't want to pay her. Skutt took exception to this and showed her independence by continuing to work at the golf course until her parents relented and agreed to match her pay at the course.

"We had pigs, chickens, cattle, llamas, goats and ponies. People loved stopping for gas and letting their kids enjoy the animals. It was interesting because we had biker gangs and all types of interesting people stop by. Summers were especially fun," Lona remembered.

In 2006 Lona graduated from Portola High School and then attended Chico State College where she earned a degree in graphic arts. "I flourished at Chico and am so glad that the sorority sisters I met there are still part of my life. I am in touch with 11 of them every day and I do mean EVERY day," she smiled.

After graduation she moved to Arizona and took a job as a waitress to pay the bills while she pursued a job search in her chosen field. No job turned up, but she did meet a "kind of shy" guy named Joel Dahmen who saw her and worked up the courage to get her phone number.

"It just felt right from the very beginning. We felt comfortable right away," Lona remembered. "But, I was headed for New York and he was headed to Canada so we agreed to try a long distance romance and see how things worked out."

Two months passed and Lona was not enjoying New York, so after the Canadian Tour ended for the season, she and Joel got back together in Scottsdale and moved in together.

"Without Lona, I might still be wallowing in self-pity and cursing my bad luck. She gave me the kick in the tail I needed to get me off my lazy butt and then supported me with unconditional love. She is special and means everything to me," Dahmen said.

Another positive is Lona has become good friends with the Bonnalies and the couples enjoy hooking up at tournaments and pleasure trips when schedules coincide. When asked about Geno, Skutt's voice softens and with obvious affection says "Geno is the most genuine person I have ever met and he and Joel are magic together. He is like family and we love him."

Geno said "We love her too. I mean that. Her devotion to Joel is so obvious and they are made for each other. We couldn't ask for a better friend."

CHAPER FIVE
BOB

In the summer of 2010, Joel and buddy Nick Taylor were getting ready to play a practice round at Gold Mountain Country Club prior to the Washington State Amateur Tournament in Bremerton, Washington. Joel would go on to dominate the event and won the tournament by a comfortable margin. But, what turned out to be far more important than the victory was meeting a man named Bob Yosaitis.

The starter that day paired Dahmen and Taylor with Brad Yosaitis who was also preparing to compete in the tournament. Bob, Brad's father, caddied for his son that day and struck up a conversation with Joel's cousin, Josh Dahmen who was on Joel's bag. The two make shift caddies became fast friends and hung out together during the tournament. The friendship continued to build and soon Joel and Bob were friends also.

As time went on, Joel became like a second son to Bob and it was Bob who was there to support him when he needed it the most.

"I was looking at Joel like he was one of my kids," said Yosaitis. 'He called me one day and was crying. I asked what was wrong and he said, "I have cancer." I told him don't worry, I'll pay for the treatment. You're getting the surgery."

"He's just a super generous guy who can and was willing to help. What he did for me was beyond belief. I had been sitting around feeling sorry for myself saying 'why me' I was pouting and deciding how hard I was willing to fight it to get back on my feet and there was Bob at my side making the treatment possible."

Dahmen fought hard enough to get back on his feet and resumed playing golf within a month of the surgery. Plus, he played well enough to qualify for the Canadian Tour in 2013.

Of course, playing on a tour takes money and once again, it was Yosaitis to the rescue. He became Dahmen's sponsor which allowed Joel to focus solely on golf.

But, Yosaitis provided more than just money. He provided true friendship and moral support. He even caddied for Dahmen on several occasions when travel costs made Geno Bonnalie's participation impractical. This included the five week South American swing of the Web.com tour.

***

Bob Yosaitis was born on June 23, 1960 to Robert and Carolyn Yosaitis in Colts Neck, New Jersey which is about 60 miles from New York City. Brother John was born two years later.

Bob's father was a banker and his mother was a teacher. They were members of the Bamn Hollow Country Club and Bob played lots of junior golf including rounds with current CBS golf announcer Jim Nance.

Bob was a good student and had his pick of colleges. He settled on Vanderbilt which met his two main criteria, academic excellence and warm weather. He graduated in 1982 with a Bachelor of Engineering degree.

Bob's first college job was in the purchasing department of Caltex petroleum in Dallas, Texas. He wanted to get a Master's Degree and tried going to night school. After a semester, he knew that wasn't going to work and, with Caltex's help, he entered the University of Michigan and got the advanced degree in 1986.

Yosaitis returned to Caltex in the Trading Department in Dallas then transferred to Bahrain, UAE where he learned the ins and outs of being a jet fuel trader. He learned his lessons well and was recruited by BHP Petroleum to open an international office.

Bob was not yet thirty but his track record was such that BHP let him pick the spot to open the office and he chose Dubai, UAE for two reasons. First, it had the infrastructure he needed to easily travel the Middle East and second it was the only place in the area that had a first-class golf course with grass greens.

At Dubai he set up all aspects of the new office and soon was trading two million barrels of jet fuel per month. This made him the largest trader in the Pacific Rim. He traveled frequently and met people at the highest levels of government because the companies where firmly controlled by the ruling classes rather the corporations.

In part because the BHP leadership feared for Yosaitis' safety due to the Iranian embargo and other unrest in the area, Bob was transferred to Singapore and became the number one trader for the company's worldwide portfolio. In 1993, the company promoted him once more and sent him to Honolulu, Hawaii to oversee all trading and marketing aspects of BHP's worldwide jet fuel operation.

Yosaitis was obviously a corporate superstar but he wanted to become and independent businessman and once again he succeeded big time. In 1998 he started Bradley Pacific Aviation and built it to a company that had 188 employees. In April of 2008, 80% of Bradley aviation was sold to Ross Aviation and in August 2014, 100% was sold to Landmark Aviation. At 48, Bob Yosaitis had become a self-made multi-millionaire.

***

While attending graduate school Bob met Chicago native Amy Brown and they were married in 1986. In 1990 son Brad was born and three years later the couple had daughter Abby. Brad is working on getting a Master's Degree at father Bob's alma mater, the University of Michigan and Abby works for a finance company in Boston.

Amy and Bob divorced and in 2016 Bob married Leinani Shak. Currently the couple lives in Las Vegas, Nevada and Bob has recently begun to play golf again. He is part owner or on the Board of Directors of four businesses.

***

Bob's son Brad went on to play golf at and graduated from Cornell University in 2013. Bob offered his son the chance to pick a trip anywhere in the world as a graduation present and Brad said, "I'll pick Canada and I'll caddie for Joel."

So, for several weeks the two young friends shared an adventure in

Canada that neither will ever forget. "I have lots of memories but two things really stick out," Yosaitis said fondly.

"First, I was on the bag when Joel was in the final group on a Sunday afternoon in the Canadian Tour Championship. We didn't win that day but the experience was thrilling and it gave me goose bumps. Second, I was with him when he shot a 61 in South America. It was unbelievable!" Yosaitis gushed.

Bob and Brad both feel strongly about Joel and they have deep respect for Bonnalie as well. "They are great young guys and I root for them every minute of every day. I think they can make it but at some point they have to step up and prove they belong in the big time. I hope they get it done," Bob said.

JOHN BLACK

CHAPTER SIX
THE LEWIS - CLARK VALLEY

The twin cities of Lewiston, Idaho and Clarkston, Washington are located 465 miles from the Pacific Ocean at the confluence of the Snake and Clearwater Rivers. The Snake serves as the Idaho – Washington border and the two cities are connected by three bridges. The joint population is about 50,000.

The Snake is part of the Columbia River system so Lewiston is actually a seaport and river transportation is an important economic factor. There is rich farm land all around the valley and agriculture is a critical part of the area's financial health and stability. At one time, the area's dominant financial driver was forestry and the Potlatch Corporation was a big player in the nation's lumber industry.

The cities are named after Meriwether Lewis and William Clark who spent time there during the exploration of the Louisiana Purchase in the early 1800's.

The river system and nearby wilderness area make Lewiston-Clarkston a hunting and fishing mecca.

The cities' valley location has an elevation of 700 feet above sea level so winters tend to be mild by northwest standards. There are many years when there is little or no snow fall and it is not unusual for the locals to play golf year around. In addition, groups of players flock to the valley from Montana, British Columbia and the Spokane area to find playable golf courses.

The Valley has four courses two public and two private. The Clarkston Country Club has been operating since 1937 and the Lewiston Country Club opened in 1927 and then changed locations in 1974. Both clubs have a long-standing and somewhat unique youth friendly attitudes and young people are encouraged to play and participate in club events. This creates a welcoming atmosphere not seen in many areas of the country. Juniors are often invited to join members for rounds at an early age and they often become the best known and most popular players in the club.

Geno Bonnalie, playing out of Lewiston, and Joel Dahmen from Clarkston grew up playing these clubs. Both began playing with a wide range of members at an early age and both were well-liked and respected by almost everyone. The memberships were proud of them and their successes.

Upon finishing college, Geno moved back to the valley after a short time working in Seattle. He secured a young adult golfing membership at the Lewiston Club. The Club's Board of Directors wanted a young person's participation and convinced him to run for a seat on the Board and he was elected easily. Quick Board turnover happened for a variety of reasons and, lo and behold, Geno found himself being the club's President at the ripe old age of 26!

He handled himself with great class and a maturity far beyond his years and further endeared himself to the club's membership. He was respected and very well-liked.

The Clarkston club has a group of men called the Boyz. At any given time there are about 25 men who play a blind draw partner's game a couple of times a week. The format promotes a wonderful camaraderie among the players and it has been going on for decades. A couple of the regulars took a liking to Joel and he was invited to join the group as a teenager. Since he was the only young person involved, he became almost like a mascot to the men involved. All liked playing golf with him.

Joel recalls his days playing with the Boyz with great warmth. "Here I was just this kid and these really cool older guys invited me to play with them. I was in heaven! To this day, some of my fondest golf memories revolve around my time with them."

The Clarkston club membership has great memories too and many have continued to follow and support Joel on his quest for fame and fortune. The 2016 Albertson's Open is a Web.com tour event in Boise, Idaho. In 2016, some 20 couples made the six hour trip from Clarkston to Boise to root for their favorite son.

***

By far, the biggest and most popular valley golf event is the Lewiston Club's Whing Ding Tournament which has been held since 1952. It attracts good players from all over the northwest for 36 holes of medal play on Saturday and Sunday of Labor Day weekend. The top 10 gross finishers qualify for the popular Sole Survivor held on Monday afternoon. All ten players tee off number one and the player with the highest score is eliminated on every hole. In the case of a tie, a chip off is held and the player furthest from the cup is the one eliminated. By the 9th hole two players are left and they go head-to-head for the title.

The event usually attracts a gallery of 300 or more and the crowd is partisan and loud in support of young local participants. Dahmen qualified five times, the first when he has 14, and won it twice. Bonnalie never won but qualified several times. Theses appearances helped solidify the two players' popularity and stature in the local golf community.

Joel and Geno were hardly unique in this way. The feats of scores of young players had been celebrated over decades by the country club communities and there had been numerous accomplished young players who dominated their peers in high school and, in some cases, college.

The big difference was Joel had succeeded in securing the grand prize – the coveted PGA card. Many locals had tried but only Joel had closed the deal. He and his pal Geno had now become full scale royalty to the valley's golf community.

So now, when Joel tees it up in competition, computers all over the Lewis-Clark Valley are tuned to pgatour.com to follow the exploits of the two popular native sons.

***

Joel Dahmen was the first Lewis-Clark Valley male to get a chance on golf's biggest stage but he was not the first person to do so. That honor belongs to Robin Walton who played junior and high school golf for Clarkston High School in the early 1970s. She was a standout on the local scene and won the Oregon Junior Championship and the Northwest Amateur in 1977. She played golf at the University of Washington, graduated from the school and then followed her dream and joined the LPGA Tour.

Robin was the LPGA's Rookie of the Year in 1979 and enjoyed a twenty-year career competing against the best women players in the world. She never won a LPGA event but she had seven top ten finishes and won nearly a million dollars in prize money.

She went on to serve three years on the LPGA Board of Directors in the early 1990s. From there she was recruited to be the Assistant Coach of the powerful Wake Forest College team and won the award as the nation's best Assistant Coach.

Some people believe Gary Floan in the 1960s or current senior and former PGA standout Kirk Triplett, were the first locals to get a PGA card. But, neither was from the Lewis-Clark Valley. Floan was from Orofino, Idaho, 40 miles from Lewiston and Triplett graduated from Pullman high School some 30 miles north.

PART TWO
THE WALK BEGINS

CHAPTER ONE
UNDERDOGS

Joel Dahmen had the coveted PGA card and a healthy optimistic outlook for the future. Caddie Geno Bonnalie was also sky high as they prepared for the next phase of their journey and the search for fame and fortune. Unfortunately, the learned very quickly that keeping the card might be harder than getting it in the first place. In a very real sense, the pair was now walking with Tigers.

The task was going to be especially tough for Joel and his role as an underdog was magnified by circumstances. He was dead last in his category because he finished twenty fifth out of twenty five on the Web.Com money list category. He could have improved his status by doing well in the Web playoff tournaments but he was unable to participate. This meant it was likely that he would get to play in fewer tournaments than most others in his class. The importance of that cannot be overstated. It would make his journey extremely difficult.

Historically, only a handful of first year players will do well enough to keep their playing privileges for a second year. The new criteria guarantees the top 125 in Fed Ex Cup points are guaranteed a spot for 2017 – 18. Most of these will be taken by established, proven players who are truly elite and have the financial freedom to play with reduced pressure and maintain a schedule comfortable to them.

These experienced, highly successful Tigers make boat loads of money both on and off the course. They have swing instructors at their beck and call. Many also have business managers, agents, fitness instructors and sports psychologists on their payrolls. They travel in a first-class manner and are able to focus all their mental energy on playing golf.

Then there is a layer of 100 or so players like Joel Dahmen who have to compete against the proven elite but have many weeks where they can't get in tournaments because they are reserved for the top players only. Also, there is a third layer of talented mini tour players, college All Americans, etc. who are highly motivated and anxious to take their spot in the big time.

***

A prime example of the extreme difficulty of making it in professional golf is the experience of Chris Williams. He grew up 30 miles from the Lewis – Clark Valley in Moscow, Idaho. Like Joel, Chris had received a scholarship to the University of Washington and had excelled beyond all expectations. In his senior college season he had risen to the lofty perch of being the number one ranked amateur in the World! By any standards this is heady stuff and Williams had the "can't miss" label.

But, even the best amateur in the world needs to prove his medal as a professional and in 2015 Williams began his own walk with Tigers by playing on the Canadian Tour. A back injury contributed to a bad start and he had to return to the Canadian Q School in order to retain his card for 2016. By midyear, he had made only five of ten cuts and was ranked 81st on the Canadian money list.

However, Chris has one big advantage over Joel – money. Because of his lofty amateur status, Nike had signed Williams to a three-year, seven figure contract. Financially he began his walk worry free. Joel, not so much.

***

Competing with the best players in the world is a hard thing to do under any circumstances but the forced weeks off magnifies the rookie's challenge immensely.

The PGA has a complicated ranking priority system that has some 300 players involved. The highest ranking players get the first chance to sign up for tournaments. These include the top 125 on the money list and those who are in the top 125 in Fed Ex points who aren't in the money category. Next, comes top ten finishers from the previous weeks, those with special exemptions like past USA Open Champions, recent tournament winners, and those with special exemptions like sponsor picks, etc. There is also a category of players who have medical deferments and four spots are always reserved for Monday qualifying at local sites.

Though somewhat confusing, the following was the exact priority list for exemption priorities at the beginning of the 2016 – 17 season:

1. Winner of PGA Championship or U.S. Open prior to 1970 or in the last five seasons and the current season:
Jack Burke, Jr.
Jason Day
Jason Dufner
Dow Finsterwald
Raymond Floyd
Doug Ford
Al Geiberger
Don January
Dustin Johnson
Brooks Koepka
Gene Littler
Rory McIlroy
Bobby Nichols
Jack Nicklaus
Gary Player
Justin Rose
Webb Simpson
Jordan Spieth
Lee Trevino
Jimmy Walker

2. Winner of THE PLAYERS Championship in the last five seasons and the current season:
Rickie Fowler
Si Woo Kim
Matt Kuchar
Tiger Woods

3. Winners of the Masters Tournament in the last five seasons and the current season:
Sergio Garcia
Adam Scott
Bubba Watson
Danny Willett

4. Winners of The Open Championship in the last five seasons and the current season:
Ernie Els
Zach Johnson
Phil Mickelson
Henrik Stenson

5. Winners of THE TOUR Championship in the last three seasons and the current season:
Billy Horschel

6. Winners of World Golf Championships events in the last three seasons and the current season:
Russell Knox
Shane Lowry
Hideki Matsuyama
Patrick Reed

7. Winners of the Arnold Palmer Invitational and the Memorial Tournament in the last three seasons and the current season, beginning with the 2015 winners.
Matt Every
Marc Leishman
David Lingmerth
William McGirt

8. Leader from the final FedEx Cup Points List in each of the last five seasons:
Brandt Snedeker

9. Leader from the final PGA TOUR Money List in each of the last five seasons:

10. Winners of PGA TOUR co-sponsored or approved tournaments, whose victories are considered official, within the last two seasons, or during the current season; winners receive an additional season of exemption for each additional win, up to five seasons:
Aaron Baddeley
Sangmoon Bae
Daniel Berger
Jonas Blixt
Steven Bowditch
Keegan Bradley
Wesley Bryan
Alex Cejka
Greg Chalmers
Kevin Chappell
Bryson DeChambeau
Tony Finau
Jim Furyk
Fabian Gomez
Branden Grace
Cody Gribble
Emiliano Grillo
Bill Haas
Adam Hadwin
James Hahn
Brian Harman
Padraig Harrington
Russell Henley
J.J. Henry

JOHN BLACK

Jim Herman
Charley Hoffman
J.B. Holmes
Mackenzie Hughes
Billy Hurley III
Smylie Kaufman
Chris Kirk
Kevin Kisner
Danny Lee
Davis Love III
Hunter Mahan
Peter Malnati
Ben Martin
Graeme McDowell
Troy Merritt
Ryan Moore
Grayson Murray
Rod Pampling
Pat Perez
Scott Piercy
D.A. Points
Jon Rahm
Xander Schauffele
Charl Schwartzel
Cameron Smith
Kyle Stanley
Brendan Steele
Robert Streb
Steve Stricker
Brian Stuard
Hudson Swafford
Vaughn Taylor
Nick Taylor
Justin Thomas
Jhonattan Vegas

11a. Players among the top 50 in career earnings as of the end of the preceding season may elect to use a one-time exemption for the next season:
Geoff Ogilvy
Carl Pettersson
Bo Van Pelt

11b. Players among the Top 25 in career earnings as of the end of the preceding season may elect to use this special one-time exemption for the next season.
Stewart Cink

12. Sponsor exemptions (a maximum of eight, which may include amateurs with handicaps of 0 or less), on the following basis:
A. Not less than two sponsor invitees shall be PGA TOUR members not otherwise exempt.
B. Not less than two of the 2016 Top Finishers of the Web.com Tour, if not all can otherwise be accommodated.
NOTE: PGA TOUR members may receive an unlimited number of sponsor invitations. Non-TOUR members may receive a maximum of seven per year.

13. Two international players designated by the Commissioner.

14. The current PGA Club Professional Champion up to 6 open events (3 must be opposite The Open Championship and World Golf Championships events), in addition to any sponsor selections.
The exemption does not apply to open, limited-field events.
Rich Berberian, Jr.

15. PGA Section Champion or Player of the Year of the Section in which the tournament is played.

16. Four low scorers at Open Qualifying which shall normally be held on Monday of tournament week.

17. Past champions of the particular event being contested that week, if cosponsored by the PGA TOUR and the same tournament sponsor, as follows:
A. Winners prior to July 28, 1970: unlimited exemptions for such events.
B. Winners after Jan. 1, 2000: five seasons of exemptions for such events.

18. Life Members (who have been active members of the PGA TOUR for 15 years and have won at least 20 co-sponsored events).
Vijay Singh
Tom Watson

19. Top 125 on the previous season's FedEx Cup points list.
Paul Casey
Gary Woodland
Roberto Castro
Sean O'Hair
Kevin Na
Jason Kokrak
Ryan Palmer
Louis Oosthuizen
Harris English
Jamie Lovemark
Charles Howell III
David Hearn
Luke Donald
Kevin Streelman
Kyle Reifers
Daniel Summerhays
Jon Curran
Ricky Barnes
Jerry Kelly
Chad Campbell
Patrick Rodgers
Harold Varner III

WALKING WITH TIGERS

Martin Laird
Johnson Wagner
Colt Knost
Scott Brown
Chez Reavie
Patton Kizzire
John Senden
Bryce Molder
Freddie Jacobson
K.J. Choi
Spencer Levin
John Huh
Sung Kang
Jason Bohn
Tyrone Van Aswegen
Derek Fathauer
Blayne Barber
Lucas Glover
Brett Stegmaier
Robert Garrigus
Zac Blair
Francesco Molinari
Cameron Tringale
Andrew Loupe
Boo Weekley
Mark Hubbard
Ben Crane
Michael Kim
Anirban Lahiri
Graham DeLaet
Luke List
Shawn Stefani
David Toms
Seung-Yul Noh

20. Top 125 on previous season's Official Money List through the Wyndham Championship
Ken Duke
Steve Marino
Bud Cauley
Retief Goosen
Chad Collins
Morgan Hoffmann

21. Players who finished greater than or equal to top 125 on the 2015-16 PGA TOUR Official Season FedEx Cup Points List or top 125 on the 2015-16 Official Season Money List through the Wyndham Championship as non-members:
Byeong Hun An
Rafa Cabrera Bello
Soren Kjeldsen

22. Major Medical Extension: If granted by the Commissioner, if not otherwise eligible, and if needed to fill the field, Special Medical Extension.
Nick Watney
Ian Poulter
Brian Gay
Patrick Cantlay
Kevin Stadler
Tim Clark
Bob Estes
Chris Couch
Ryo Ishikawa
Troy Kelly
Briny Baird
Harrison Frazar
Charlie Beljan
John Peterson

23. Leading Money Winner from the previous season's Top 25 regular season players using combined money earned on the Official Web.com Tour Regular Season Money List and Web.com Tour Finals Money List, Leading Money Winner from the previous season's Web.com Tour Finals and Three-Time Winners from previous season Web.com Tour.

24. Leading money winner from Web.com Tour medical

25. Top 10 and ties, not otherwise exempt, among professionals from the previous open tournament whose victory has official status are exempt into the next open tournament whose victory has official status.

26. Top Finishers of the Web.com Tour:
Finishers 2-25 from the previous season's Top 25 Web.com Tour Regular season players using combined money earned on the Web.com Tour Regular Season Money List and money earned in the Web.com Tour Finals and the top 25 players and ties on the Web.com Tour Finals Money List at the conclusion of the Finals who are not already exempt.
Kelly Kraft
Kevin Tway
Ollie Schniederjans
Whee Kim
C.T. Pan
J.J. Spaun
Dominic Bozzelli
Ryan Blaum
Scott Stallings
Trey Mullinax
J.T. Poston
Brandon Hagy
Michael Thompson
Cameron Percy
Seamus Power
Sebastian Munoz
Jonathan Randolph

Rick Lamb
Martin Flores
Rory Sabbatini
Richy Werenski
Julian Etulain
Tim Wilkinson
Ryan Brehm
Andres Gonzales
Brian Campbell
Joel Dahmen
Will MacKenzie
Tag Ridings
Gonzalo Fdez-Castano
Mark Anderson
Nicholas Lindheim
Steven Alker
Andrew Johnston
Ryan Armour
Brett Drewitt
Miguel Angel Carballo
Brad Fritsch
Zack Sucher
Bobby Wyatt
Max Homa
Brian Davis
Kris Blanks
Will Claxton
Lee Williams
Shane Bertsch
David Berganio, Jr.

Note: Reordered after the conclusion of The RSM Classic and the Genesis Open; thereafter, Mondays of the Masters, THE PLAYERS Championship, U.S. Open and The Open Championship.

27. Top Finishers from the Web.com Tour medical:
NOTE: This category will be reordered with the above category #26.

28. Players winning three Web.com Tour events in the current season:

29. Minor medical extension:

30. Twenty-five finishers beyond 125th place on prior season's FedEx Cup Points List (126-150):
Matt Jones
Sam Saunders
Chris Stroud
Greg Owen
Steve Wheatcroft
Tom Hoge
Willy Wilcox
Hiroshi Iwata
Tyler Aldridge
Stuart Appleby
Bronson Burgoon
Nicholas Thompson
S.J. Park
Note: Reordered after the conclusion of The RSM Classic and the Genesis Open; thereafter, Mondays of the Masters, THE PLAYERS Championship, U.S. Open and The Open Championship.

31. Nonexempt, major medical/family crisis:
NOTE: This category will be reordered with the above category #30.

32. Reorder Categories 33-37
Camilo Villegas
Thomas Pieters
Tyrrell Hatton
Tommy Fleetwood
Jonathan Byrd

Bill Lunde
Angel Cabrera
Andres Romero
Jason Gore
Ross Fisher
Fred Couples
Mark Wilson
Chesson Hadley
Brendon de Jonge
Y.E. Yang
Dicky Pride
Ted Potter, Jr.
John Merrick
Charlie Wi
Larry Mize
Michael Bradley
Tommy Gainey
Arjun Atwal
Justin Leonard
Troy Matteson
George McNeill
Tim Petrovic
Tim Herron
Eric Axley
Brendon Todd
Fred Funk
John Rollins
Robert Allenby
Craig Barlow

Note: Categories 33-37 Reordered after the conclusion of The RSM Classic and the Genesis Open; thereafter, Mondays of the Masters, THE PLAYERS Championship, U.S. Open and The Open Championship.

33. Past Champions, Team Tournament Winners and Veteran Members Beyond 150 on the FedEx Cup Points List:
If not otherwise eligible and as needed to fill the field, Past Champion members, Team Tournament Winners and Veteran members beyond 150th place on the previous season's FedEx Cup Points List in order of their combined official PGA TOUR and Web.com Tour earnings in the previous season.

Jeff Overton
D.J. Trahan
Derek Ernst
Marc Turnesa
Bernhard Langer
Cameron Beckman
Ted Purdy
Billy Mayfair
Steve Flesch
Rocco Mediate
Frank Lickliter II
Mark O'Meara
Trevor Immelman
Marco Dawson
Shaun Micheel
Rich Beem
Mark Hensby
Peter Lonard
Ben Curtis
Chris Smith
Len Mattiace
Kent Jones
Omar Uresti
Matt Bettencourt
Richard S. Johnson
Brett Wetterich

34. Past Champion Members: If not otherwise eligible and if needed to fill the field, Past Champion members, in order of the total number of cosponsored or approved events won, excluding Team events.

If two or more players are tied, the player who is higher on the PGA Tour Career Money List shall be eligible.

35. Special Temporary Members: If during the course of a PGA TOUR season, a nonmember of the PGA TOUR wins an amount of points (e.g., by playing in PGA TOUR events through sponsor exemptions, Open Qualifying, etc.) equal to the amount won in the preceding season by the 150th finisher on the FedExCup points list, he will be eligible to become a special temporary member for the remainder of the season.

36. Team Tournament Winners: If not otherwise eligible and if needed to fill the field, winners of co-sponsored team championships, in order of the total number of team championship tournaments won.

If two or more players are tied based on the number of such tournaments won, the player who is higher on the official PGA TOUR Career Money List shall be eligible.

37. Veteran Members: If not otherwise eligible and if needed to fill the field, Veteran members (players who have made a minimum of 150 cuts during their career), in order of their standing on the PGA Tour Career Money List.

So, improving one's position and getting into enough tournaments to successfully compete is a very big deal. But, there are other disadvantages. For rookies, every PGA golf course is a new adventure and they must get as much local knowledge as possible in a very short time. The top players usually play in a Wednesday Pro-Am which means they have at least two full days to adjust to a new course. Rookies seldom get an invitation to the Pro-Am so basically they have one day to learn the quirks associated with a particular golf course.

Add these factors up and the difficulty of surviving a rookie season becomes obvious. Some will do it. But, most will not.

***

WALKING WITH TIGERS

In 2013 the PGA made a major change to an old custom and eliminated Q-School as a way for a player to get PGA privileges. The Q-School method had begun in 1965 and lasted nearly five decades. Q-School provided tour cards for players that had fallen out of the top 125, graduating college players, talented foreign players and, very importantly, dreamers. Anyone with a scratch handicap and entry fee money could attempt to play their way onto golf's biggest stage.

The format was grueling. The tournament was six, eighteen hole rounds that tested the players mentally and physically as they moved in and out of the top 30 spots on the leaderboard. It was truly unique because it brought college stars and dreamers into direct competition with journeymen professionals trying to earn a card for another season.

The six-round format was designed to prevent a player from making the tour simply because they caught lightning in a bottle for a couple of days. Additionally, the six-round format was the finals. To get there, a player would have to get through two other stages of Regional Qualifying which are full of talented golfers.

Because of the drama filled history of Q-School, there was many vocal opponents to the changes made. One key concern was that hot shots coming out of college could no longer waltz on the PGA Tour by placing in the top 30 of a qualifying event. Now such players would have to spend a year on the Web.com Tour.

***

The Q-School decision put the Web.com Tour on the map in a way never experienced previously. It now became the single most important element of getting to golf's big leagues.

Joel Dahmen got his card in the new traditional way by finishing in the top 25 on the Web.com Tour money list. Joel was the 25th qualifier on the list so he entered the year near the very bottom of the pecking order in his particular classification.

This is important because tour events have a maximum of 156 spots so players in higher classifications (noted above) get to compete in the most popular tournaments before entries are open to people like Joel. This makes it very hard for rookies and lower ranked players because sometimes they go several weeks without getting in a chance to play in a PGA event. This also intensifies the pressure to succeed on those occasions when the player does get the opportunity to compete with the tigers.

Every four weeks, the PGA shuffles the priority list based on performance so four September tournaments provided a golden opportunity for Joel to improve his standing. Unfortunately, that didn't happen.

The week after locking up the card, Joel and Geno came home to the Lewis-Clark Valley to visit family and friends and share in the festivities surrounding the Lewiston club's Whing Ding event. They were greeted like conquering heroes and people were standing in line to buy them an adult beverage and wish them well. It was a happy time for Joel, Geno and their many friends. The two even participated in the tournament's Mixed Chapman event with Holly and Lona as their partners.

Unfortunately, sometimes bad things happen to good people and Joel slipped on the club's driving range and broke two bones in his hand. He was unable to swing a club for over a month. The injury could not have come at a worse time. His underdog role suddenly went up several more notches because he could not participate in the playoff system that could have improved his playing status.

Still, despite the odds, the historical failure of others, and the injury-plagued slow start, a couple of things seemed to be in Dahmen's favor.

***

The first reason to be encouraged was the performance of long-time friend and competitor Nick Taylor. Nick and Joel were roommates in Seattle when both were playing for the University of Washington. They had also been in junior golf together and had gone head-to-head on many occasions. Joel had more than held his own in these competitions and which one is actually the better player is a day-to-day, variable thing.

Nick earned his PGA card in 2015 and shocked people by winning in his fourth start on tour! He earned over a million dollars that year and followed that up with $628,000 in winnings in 2016.

"I'm excited for Joel and I'm excited that he is going to be out here with me. He has been through so much with his mom's death and the struggles with his game. It is a testament to him and his courage that he never gave up on his dream," Taylor said.

Nick also commented on Joel's ability. "He is a pure ball striker and those of us who know him know how good he can be."

Dahmen sees the success of Taylor as an affirmation of his own potential. "If Nick can do it, so can I," he commented.

The second asset is Joel has a natural golf swing and he is considered to be a tremendous ball striker with effortless power. This cannot be over stated because today's PGA golf courses are very long and most require great precision. Joel's statistics on the Canadian and Web.com tours prove he has the ball striking skill to compete at the highest level. His driving distance, driving accuracy and greens in regulation numbers were among the very best.

The other asset is a seemingly mature outlook and perspective of golf's place in life. Joel often commented that golf is what he does It "is not who I am." Caddie Geno and girlfriend Lona have both been amazed at how easily Joel can put a bad round behind him.

"He usually doesn't take a bad round home with him – he leaves it at the course," Lona said.

Joel expresses it more distinctly. "I have seen life and death and golf isn't it."

This approach would likely serve him well when the pressure of PGA golf became a reality. This mindset was about to be tested as the first step of his walk with the Tigers was about to happen.

CHAPTER TWO
THE OPENER

THURSDAY OCTOBER 27, 2016
JACKSON COUNTRY CLUB
JACKSON, MISSISSIPPI
1:29 PM

Jackson, Mississippi is the state's capital and the metropolitan area is home to around 500,000 people. It was named for Andrew Jackson honoring him for his command role in the War of 1812. Later, Jackson would serve as the nation's seventh President of the United States.

The area has hosted a PGA tour stop since 1968. It was originally held at the Hattiesburg Country Club and later moved to the Annadale Golf Club where it stayed through 2013. At that point, Sanderson Farms took over as corporate sponsor and the tournament was moved to its current home, the Jackson Country Club.

So here, in the heart of the south, Joel Dahmen and Geno Bonnalie made their way to the first tee of their first PGA event amid a boat load of nervous anticipation, sweaty palms and butterflies. Despite this, Joel's first drive was a 310 yard rocket, center cut. A wedge and two putts followed and their first hole on the PGA Tour was a cozy par.

Dahmen had made it into the Jackson field, because all of golf's biggest names were either not playing this week or had been enticed to enter the 9.5 million dollar World Golf Championship in Shanghai, China. Still, the Sanderson Farms Championship had a 4.5 million dollar purse and a field that included such notables as Ian Poulter, Angel Cabrera, Geoff Ogilvy, two time US Open Champion Retief Goosen, Lucas Glover, Ben Curtis, David

Toms and former number one in the World Rankings, David Duval. The tourney looked and felt like the big time especially with the Golf Channel's coverage team on site and highly visible.

The hospitality and food were superb and Dahmen was able to play a practice round with his old buddy Nick Taylor and PGA veteran Dicky Pride, a past PGA tournament champion. Further, while hitting balls on the practice tee, Joel and Geno were joined by Goosen and Duval. "Pretty heady stuff for a couple of kids from Idaho," Bonnalie joked.

"Plus, we had the neatest lunch ever. This great seafood restaurant set up a buffet on the driving range and I ate smoked oysters and Cajun until I was totally stuffed. On the Web Tour caddies were lucky to get a free hot dog," Geno added.

***

The PGA tour has a somewhat elitist format when it comes to player pairings for its events. It's a four-tier system that breaks down roughly like this:

1) Major championship winners, recent tournament winners, top 30 on the career money list.
2) Tournament winners or other names of note.
3) Career non-winners who are in the top 125 on the money list, have at least $750,000 in career earnings or are in the top 50 in World Rankings.
4) All others including Web.com money list qualifiers, Monday qualifiers or those who have received a sponsor's exemption.

Those in the number one pairings get the most desirable tee times, in the middle of the morning and afternoon sessions. The group three and four players get only the very first, or more commonly, the very last times in the two blocks. This often makes things a bit harder because the greens tend to be drier and faster and the course is often full of divots on the fairways and spike marks on the greens.

These factors contribute to the underdog role of the non- established players like Dahmen but it is a reality that must be faced and overcome if a player is to reach the upper echelon of professional golf.

Joel and Geno were obviously in the fourth pairing category as were his playing companions Brad Fritsch and Brian Rowell. Fritsch is a 39 year- old Canadian who is currently 349th in the World Rankings. Like Dahmen, he earned his card for his performance on the Web.com Tour where he was 16th on the money list. This included one victory and one runner-up finish in the 2016 tournaments. His most notable career achievement was an 8th place finish in the PGA's Wyndham Championship in 2014.

Rowell is a native Mississippian who played college golf at Ole Miss and got in the event by the playing in the Monday qualifier.

***

Dahmen parred the first five holes which wasn't a disastrous start but it wasn't good either. Two of those holes are par 5's and, the field as a whole was overpowering them. Not taking advantage of number five seemed to frustrate Joel and he took a double bogey 6 on the next hole. Another bogey was made at the ninth and he made the turn with a very disappointing 39. This was frustrating because conditions were perfect and a many of the pros were posting low scores.

Things went better on the back nine and the 2 under 34 resulted in a 73. Fritsch had carded a 71 and Rowell an even par 72. This is where one has to view the round like a glass of water - half full or half empty.

On one hand, Joel's scored placed him in 101st position a whopping 10 shots behind defending champion and first round leader Keith Steelman who posted a sparkling 63.

However, because of the smaller than normal field and the fact that a few other players had also struggled, the projected cut was 2 under par. This meant Dahmen would have to post a very achievable 69 in the second round to have a reasonable chance of making the cut and earning a check in his very first PGA tournament.

***

On Tuesday afternoon Joel and Geno were messing around the event's practice putting green. Joel was trying out various putters because he was beginning to lose confidence in his Taylor Made. The Odyssey two-ball felt good and he drained some putts with it that afternoon and again on Wednesday when the two players had played a money game against PGA pros Cameron Beckman and Chris Smith. (The match ended all square).

"We decided it couldn't hurt to put the Odyssey in play on Thursday and it might have been a mistake," Bonnalie said. "Joel hit the ball well but wasn't able to convert a lot of the putts he normally makes. He lost 3.7 shots to the field in putting and another 1.5 in chipping. It was just one of those days."

"It looks like we need a 68 tomorrow to get safely inside the cut line. I'm not even worried about it. We just need a couple of putts to fall and that number will be easy," Geno predicted.

***

Bonnalie looked like a seer early in the round. With his old putter back in the bag, Dahmen started with a bogey on his opening hole, the 10th, but then went on a birdie run with four in a row on holes 13 through 16 which led to a solid 33. Another birdie on number three put him four under par with six holes to play. The coveted 68 was very much in sight as was the badly needed paycheck. Then it all came apart.

Suddenly Joel began to hit poor iron shots. This put him in a position where he had to depend on his putting to save pars and he didn't cope well. Three putts on holes 6, 7 and 9 resulted in bogeys and, what looked to be a good round turned into a disappointing 71. Making the cut seemed impossible and sure enough he missed it by two shots. A 69 would have done the trick.

After the round Bonnalie was "experiencing the worst feeling a caddie can have." On number 8, the groups' second to last hole, Geno had mixed up two sprinkler heads and had given Dahmen an incorrect distance. This resulted in Joel's second shot coming up 20 yards short. He saved par with a good chip but the conscientious Bonnalie was beating himself up pretty bad. To Joel's credit he handled the mistake with class and the next morning Bonnalie was feeling better especially when he was reminded that it was Joel, not him, who had putted like a dog the entire weekend.

The PGA statistics told the whole story. In the two rounds, Dahmen had lost six shots to the field in chipping and putting.

Meanwhile, Joel's old roommate Nick Taylor fired two rounds of 68 and was only two shots behind co-leaders Greg Owen and Grayson Murray. He faded a bit from there but finished tied for 23rd and won $40,320. Playing partner Rowell matched Dahmen and also missed the cut but, Fritsch rallied for a 68 and made the cut with a stroke to spare. He cashed a check for $26,705, tying for 29th.

***

WINNER'S CIRCLE – Cody Gribble fired a seven under par 65 which included a blistering 31 on the back nine to win the tournament by four shots. This was a huge deal for Gribble who had spent the last two seasons on the Web.com Tour as a peer of Joel Dahmen. They entered the tournament with the same exempt classification.

Of course, this was Gribble's first PGA win which comes as no surprise because in four of the past six years the Sanderson Farms Championship has produced a first time winner. What was surprising is that Gribble overcame a poor start, recovering from a 73 opening day score before rallying with rounds of 63, 67 and 65.

Gribble paid special tribute to his caddie Bobby Hudson who "stayed in my ear the whole time and it was rarely about yardage or club selection. He helped me stay in the present. There was no looking at scoreboards or thinking ahead to the next hole. He was able to keep me patient and motivated," Gribble said.

First place finishes are golden for rookies. Gribble raked in a healthy $756,000 and no longer had to worry about being on the bottom of the PGA exemption pecking order. The victory won him a full two year exemption for future tournaments.

CHAPTER THREE

SATURDAY, OCTOBER 29, 2016
LAS VEGAS, NEVADA

Geno Bonnalie was thrilled to get out of Jackson. Not only had the golf been disappointing but he had shared a room with two other caddies in "the sleaziest place I have ever been in."

"The place was filthy, the carpet was ripped, the showerhead was broken, and we didn't get fresh linen. I would have complained but I was afraid I would have been shot or knifed for being a smart-assed Yankee. The good thing is it only cost $220 for the week and we split that three ways." Bonnalie joked. "Joel and Lona stayed in a first-class hotel that probably cost that much per night."

Now Geno was in Las Vegas where he was the guest of Bob Yosaitis who owns a high rise condo with a beautiful view of the strip. Joel and Lona would also be enjoying Yosaitis' hospitality so the lodging, food and drink were going to be first-class!

The downside was Dahmen did not get in the week's field because Las Vegas is one of the most popular tour stops of the year. He would have to get in via Monday qualifying, the absolute toughest task on the PGA Tour. Some 120 players would be playing 18 holes and only four of them would get into the tournament.

The hope of this happening was dashed immediately. On the second hole, Dahmen hit the wrong ball incurring a two-stroke penalty and things went downhill from there. Officially, he logged in an nc (no card) and that was that.

CHAPTER FOUR

OCTOBER 31, 2016
MEXICO CITY, MEXICO

The following Monday, Dahmen and Skutt made their way to Mexico City for another Monday qualifier for the GHL Classic at Mayakoba. Bonnalie returned to Lewiston because the expense involved didn't justify the long shot odds of getting into the field and his decision proved to be a wise one. Dahmen shot and uninspiring 70 four shots shy of qualifying.

The expenses were piling up with no checks coming in to offset them. This made the winter's final event in Sea Island, Georgia even more compelling. Joel was nearly broke and had not earned a check of any kind for almost six months.

Dahmen's slump was also affecting Bonnalie who earns a weekly salary of $1500 at PGA events but must pay his own expenses. Airfare from Lewiston or Spokane is costly and motel, rental car and meals for a week generally eat up almost all of the salary. Geno also gets the standard caddy fee of 7.5% of his player's winnings but, with no money coming in, this had been a non-issue for months.

The problem is further complicated by the presence of Lona who was now traveling to all of the events with Dahmen. On the Web.com Tour, Joel and Geno had a deal where Geno would pay for the car and Joel would cover motel costs. Now lodging was solely Geno's responsibility.

This made saving money where he could mandatory. Geno was always looking to cut expenses resulting in finding cheap flights, bunking wherever he could and sometimes sleeping in his car in the middle of a multi stop travel routine.

Lona's continuing presence was also taking a personal toll on Bonnalie.

WALKING WITH TIGERS

He was often the "third man out" for social events, meals and general tourism time during the non-golf course hours. Now, instead of hanging out and enjoying time with his best friend, he was often alone.

Broke and alone are not ingredients for happiness. But, Geno's love of golf and unconditional belief in Joel were keeping him going.

CHAPTER FIVE

SEA ISLAND, GEORGIA
NOVEMBER 17 – 18

Living in Lewiston, Idaho has many benefits. Convenience of travel is not one of them. Lewiston does have a regional airport of sorts but the flight options are limited and usually quite expensive. There are two non-stop flights per day to Seattle via Alaska Air and three more to Salt Lake City via Delta but, if these two places are not one's final destination, they are simply starting points requiring connections, plane changes, etc.

A standing joke among locals is if you want to fly east from Lewiston you first fly west, and then six hours later, you fly back over Lewiston finally headed in the right direction. Sadly, this is not just peculiar it is often true.

Also, "deals" are rarely available so the budget conscious usually have to drive two and-a-half hours northwest to Spokane, Washington to find decent and affordable flight options. Since Geno Bonnalie is "thrifty", his trips often include numerous connections some which require him to leave Lewiston by car at three am. Sometimes he spends the night before his flight with Holly's parents in nearby Post Falls but even that presents a challenge so naps in grocery store parking lots or on airport floors are commonplace. This is all part of the "Lewiston Flightmare".

Geno faced this typical flightmare getting to the PGA season's final event the RSM Classic in Sea Island, Georgia. He started his trip on Saturday the 12th because Joel was scheduled to play in Monday's Pro- Am and he needed to be on site Sunday night. He drove to Spokane, flew to Seattle, flew to Charlotte, flew to Jacksonville and rented a car to drive to Sea Island. He arrived at midnight and spent the night in his car at a Kia Sol parking lot.

He also had spent the night in a parking lot on his way to the first tournament in Mississippi.

Now in Georgia and refreshed from his parking lot nap, Geno spent Sunday enjoying a round of golf with a local caddie friend he had met on the Web.com Tour. The other good news was Dahmen had rented a house for the week with old-time friend Nick Taylor so Geno was spared the indignity of another weekly stay in a dangerous flop house similar to the room in Mississippi.

As it turned out, Joel didn't get in the Pro-Am after all so Monday, Tuesday and Wednesday were spent getting ready for the tournament by playing practice rounds with Taylor and Web.com friends Kelly Kraft and John Randolph. It was a good few days, Joel was playing well and he loved their tournament pairing with close friend Nick Lindheim and an up and comer Michael Johnson, who had almost won his first tour start at the Barbosal a few weeks earlier. They were brimming with confidence and looking forward to a great week.

In an interview in the Lewiston Morning Tribune Joel shared his feelings. "It is neat to be out here. I mean, Luke Donald has the locker next to mine and seeing the likes of Jim Furyk, Ernie Els and Zach Johnson just a few stools away is definitely different, but it's just golf. The ball is still round and a 7-iron is still a 7-iron. I do feel like I belong and hopefully I can prove that."

***

Sea Island, Georgia is in southeast Georgia 90 miles from Jacksonville, Florida. It has a colorful history and in the early 1900s it was "the in place" to go for the rich and famous from the New York metropolitan area. Many of the city's high society spent some of their winter on the island and the likes of New York Mayor Jimmy Walker, Eddie Rickenbacher, Edsel Ford and John D. Rockefeller were frequent visitors.

The PGA golf tournament was started as the McGladery Classic in 2010, and in 2015 it was changed to the RSM Classic played at the Sea Island Golf Club. Davis Love III grew up in the area and serves as the tournament's ambassador and host.

***

Dahmen shot a rock solid five under par 66 in the event's first round. This was four shots off the lead but he was in a tie for 41st place which was well within the projected cut line of three under. "He made it look easy today. He can go a lot lower tomorrow and I'm excited," Bonnalie gushed.

In Friday's second round Dahmen struggled from the start. He wasn't hitting anything solid and had very few legitimate birdie putts. Still, he was even through 11 holes and still very much under the cut line when the wheels came off once again. He doubled the 12th when his second shot buried under the lip of a bunker and he had to pitch out sideways. He followed that up with three-putt bogies on 14 and 16.

The end result was another missed cut by one stroke which meant no check for player or caddie. Playing companion Michael Johnson also missed the cut by shooting 72 – 71 but Nick Lindlem finished 54th and made $13,800.

The similarities between this tournament and the one in Mississippi are impossible to ignore. In both events, Joel had the cut made easily with nine holes to play only to throw both opportunities away with a series of three putts and poor chipping. Statistics tell the tale. In Mississippi he lost 6 shots to the field in putting/chipping and at Sea island it was a full 4 shots.

Now he was looking at several weeks off before he would be able to get in another PGA event because he was not eligible for the three tournaments scheduled in December. The work to be done during this break was painfully obvious.

The truth is it is tough being on the PGA circuit. The Tigers don't make mistakes like the players on lesser tours so there is no wiggle room for mistakes or "do-overs". Joel and Geno had been a part of only two tournaments but already they were seeing the enormous challenge ahead of them.

***

WINNER'S CIRCLE – 25 year-old Canadian Mackenzie Hughes holed an 18-foot par putt from off the green to win the tournament and became the second rookie to garner a victory early in this PGA season. Like Cody Gribble in the Sanderson Farm event, the win was huge career boost for Hughes. He took home $1,000,800 and earned a two year exemption to boot.

Hughes actually led the tournament after each of the first three rounds but still had to survive a playoff that started on Sunday night but wasn't concluded until Monday morning. The ending was rather bizarre.

Hughes was the only one of the remaining four playoff players to miss the green with his tee shot on the par three 17th hole. He thought he had to hole his 18 footer to stay in the playoff and "I made the putt of my life," he exclaimed. Then things got quite strange.

Blayne Barber, Henrik Nolander and Camilo Villegas all missed putts inside of ten feet and Hughes was champion.

CHAPTER SIX

DECEMBER, 2016
SCOTTSDALE, ARIZONA

Joel made some good decisions in early December and spent the month getting ready for what he hoped would be a productive and profitable January.

First of these was a subtle shift in scheduling priorities. Upon earning the PGA card Dahmen and caddie Geno Bonnalie had established time priorities as follows: 1) Enter the PGA events that had room for Joel 2) Monday qualifying for PGA events 3) Enter Web.com events if options one and two were not possible.

Sponsor and friend Bob Yosaitis convinced them to swap the second and third priorities because Monday qualifying was almost always a losing proposition and Web.com tournaments offered a much better chance to stay tournament sharp and earn some badly needed money. The downside is Web.com tournaments are not a cost effective for Bonnalie. His salary for these tournaments is $800 per week which is barely enough to cover his travel expenses. Plus, the payouts are such that paying a caddie is not prudent for Dahmen.

So it was agreed that Brad Yosaitis, Bob's son, would step in and carry the bag on some occasions when Web events became the best alternative. Bob would cover all of Brad's travel expenses and Joel would eliminate caddie fees.

Second, Dahmen signed a contract with Taylor Made to use their woods which put a few badly needed guaranteed dollars in the bank account and helped ease the burden of travel expenses.

Third, Dahmen began working with Cool Clubs Golf a club fitting and technology company in Scottsdale. Their camera settings caught a putting flaw and he began to make the set up and stroke changes to correct it.

Basically, the camera showed that Joel's forward stroke often left the putter head open at impact. Ironically, Joel's contact at Cool Guys is Chris Thomas, whose father Craig had been the Lewiston Country Club's head professional for many years. Chris grew up at the Lewiston Club and was a very successful junior player. He had also tried various mini tours before becoming a well-respected golf swing analyst.

Fourth, Dahmen spend countless hours perfecting wedge play with TPC Scottsdale teaching professional Rob Rashell. For hours on end he would hit lobs, knock down shots, fades and draws from 125 yards and under. His confidence in executing these shots was growing daily.

All of this had created in Joel a restless eagerness to get back on the tournament trail. The downside was it was beginning to look like his January and February PGA opportunities were shrinking rapidly due to his low standing in the PGA rankings.

The first event of 2017 is the SBS Tournament of Champions in Kapalua, Hawaii. Only those players who won an event in 2016 were invited to participate. Next up was the Sony Open on Oahu. This tournament has filled up for more than a decade and there was never a chance Dahmen would get into the field.

When the two Hawaii tournaments are completed, the PGA tour shifts to a series of attractive and popular venues on the west coast.

The first of the California tournaments is the Farmers Insurance Open in Palm Springs during the final week of January. (The old Bob Hope Tournament) Though popular, Joel and Geno had this one firmly marked on their calendars because three courses are used making a larger field possible. Unfortunately, the PGA recently cut this event's field from 180 to 156 players and this made the Dahmen – Bonnalie team questionable. As of January 6th, they were on the bubble at 156th on the eligible list and several players rated ahead of them still had two weeks to submit an entry.

The bad news kept flowing when Tiger Woods announced he would make his 2017 debut by playing at Torrey Pines the week after the Palm Springs tournament. This temporarily bounced Dahmen who had been sitting on the final spot. Usually a few players drop out for a variety of reasons the week before the tournament but the odds of getting in seemed slim. This news was a real gut punch to Joel and Geno. In past years, players with Joel's rating had gotten to compete at Torrey Pines because two courses were used and the field was expanded. Not this time. What appeared to be a certain opportunity to compete now was up in the air.

The Waste Management tournament in Scottsdale and the Genesis Open at Riviera are definitely sell outs and Joel and Geno were never counting on getting to play in them. This left only the AT & T at Monterey (the old Bing Crosby) as a tournament they are assured of getting in. The reason for this is many top players skip this event because they don't like the six hour rounds that come with three days of Pro-Am play plus the weather in the area can be raw in February.

So, despite the long odds, Monday qualifying was beginning to look like the only option of earning an entry for at least two and possibly four of the west coast tournaments.

Crawling into the top 125 in the PGA FedEx Cup standings is a daunting task under any circumstances. With few opportunities to play it becomes almost impossible. The apparent lack of playing options was beginning to take its toll on everyone and friction was developing.

No tournament income had been earned in months and both the Dahmen and Bonnalie households were struggling. This was stressing everyone and tempers were short. Dahmen wrote an ugly text to Bonnalie because of a text Geno had send to Lona about their chances of getting in the Torrey Pines event. Geno responded in kind and the two quit speaking for a time. As a matter of fact, the two who once spoke by phone nearly every day, were now communicating weekly or less. Plus, when they did speak the old warmth was gone. The dear friends were not getting along at all.

Lona Skutt was having serious doubts about quitting her job and running up travel expenses when no money was coming in and her stress was weighing on Dahmen. Even the ever upbeat and optimistic Holly Bonnalie was beginning to question the situation. The August joy of getting the PGA card was turning into something far different.

CHAPTER SEVEN

SANDALS EMERALD BEACH
BAHAMAS
JANUARY 8 – 11

The beautiful Sandals Resort. Pearly white beaches, swaying palm trees, eye popping scenery. Heaven on earth. Or, maybe not.

Most of the world's top golfers were playing in Hawaii and Bob Yosaitis had convinced Joel Dahmen to play in the Web.com event in the Bahamas and had made good on his promise to provide son Brad to serve as caddie for the week.

The entire week was survival of the fittest and the records broken were not of the positive variety. Sunday's opening round had two separate wind delays as conditions were all but unplayable with sustained winds of forty miles per hour and gusts much higher. Play had to be suspended because balls were literally being blown off some of the more exposed greens.

When round one was finally completed on Monday afternoon there were several scores in the 90's and the average score was a whopping 80.41, the highest in Web.com history. As the week progressed the winds subsided a little bit but the second round average score was still a hearty 78.2. The cut line was 11 over, also the highest in Web.com history.

Joel Dahmen, with Brad Yosaitis on the bag, shot a respectable first round of 76 and followed that with a 75 in round two. This easily made the cut and assured Joel of a check for the first time since July. He was tied for 31st when he teed it up for round three.

"The weather delays and slow play caused by the wind was brutal. We got in only five holes on Sunday and then had to go a grueling 31 holes on Monday. The wind was relentless and by Monday night we were exhausted."

Said Yosaitis.

Tuesday's third round was not much easier and by day's end, Joel had completed five holes when play was suspended due to darkness. He had fallen to 54th position mostly because of a dreaded snowman 8 on his second to the last hole of the day. On that hole, Dahmen's tee shot landed in the ocean and then he had to gut out the rest of the distance in what Yosaitis described as "brutal conditions".

Wednesday was the last day of the tournament and once again Dahmen was required to grind out 31 holes. Still, it proved to be a great day for a couple of reasons. The wind was still a tough factor but Dahmen completed round three with no further damage and then shot an impressive 70 over his final 18 holes to climb up to 21st place. This earned him a badly needed $6800 check. This didn't cure his financial woes by any means but it did provide some affirmation that Joel's game was headed in the right direction.

Better yet, Geno Bonnalie had heard from a friend and learned they were off the bubble and assured a place in the field of the Career Builder tournament in Palm Springs beginning January 19th. Things were looking up and Joel and Geno were speaking again.

CHAPTER EIGHT

LEWISTON, IDAHO

Geno Bonnalie made his flight reservations for Palm Springs and was able to avoid the "Lewiston Flightmare" by booking an inexpensive flight directly from Lewiston to San Diego where he would rent a car and make the short drive to Palm Springs. No curling up in the back seat in grocery store parking lots on this trip!

But, lodging was still an issue as he had no desire to repeat the flea bag, caddie sharing experience of Mississippi. So, he had a brain storm and decided to run with it. He put an ad on Craig's List seeking a host family which is fairly normal on the Web.com Tour. He was immediately contacted by a man who said he had a room at the Hyatt that he would be glad to make available.

He followed up with Geno and asked if Geno could get him some "golf stuff" from the tournament. Geno said sure and promised to bring some balls, hats or gloves. The guy wrote back and said he was hoping for golf clubs. When Geno wrote back and said he couldn't make that happen the guy wrote again and said "good luck" with no offer to make good on the promised room.

The next person to contact Bonnalie said he had a nice place near the host course and he would be happy to have Geno use his spare bedroom. Geno thanked him and the guy sent a text saying he was gay and did that bother Geno? He replied "no, that's not a problem." Within a few minutes the guy sent back a nude text picture of himself in a very provocative pose.

"Maybe Craig's List wasn't my best idea," Bonnalie joked.

Luckily, Holly Bonnalie got in touch with Geno's long lost Aunt Silvia who welcomed Geno with open arms. "She was a real cool lady who had great family stories. We opened a bottle of wine almost every night and laughed a lot. "She was a great hostess! Most fun I have had in a long time," Geno said.

CHAPTER NINE

LA QUINTA, CALIFORNIA
JANUARY 23 – 28, 2017

"I so belong out here. I'm living the dream," wrote Geno Bonnalie after his first day in the Palm Springs area for the Career Builders Challenge Golf Tournament. "Being out here with people I have idolized is something so special it's almost unreal."

Geno's enthusiasm stemmed from a practice range session where Joel Dahmen was hitting balls next to Geoff Ogilvy, Boo Weekley and Charles Howell III. Better yet, Joel had just finished a practice round where he putted with a new found confidence and soundly trounced fellow competitor Adam Hadwin. This led Bonnalie to gush "I feel great about what we are going to do this week!"

Bonnalie's words show his dedication to his role as a caddie but his actions speak even louder. Though he doesn't like to discuss it, Geno literally "plays in pain" almost every day. Two years ago he was struck with Plantar Fasciitis, a disease that results in pain in the heel and bottom of the feet. The disease hits about 10% of people sometime in their lives and it usually goes away with time. The best remedy for improvement is rest and staying off one's feet. This is hardly possible for a caddie.

This means Bonnalie often has lots of pain late in rounds and sometimes every step he takes on the back nine is painful. Despite this, he never complains and carries on day after day with nary a whisper about his painful condition.

Some people really do love what they do for a living. Geno is exhibit A.

***

Unfortunately, the optimism of the great practice was squashed on the very first day of the event. The Career Builder is played on three different golf courses and the cut is made after 54 holes rather than the traditional 36 holes. It is also a three day Pro-Am, a left over tradition from the days when the tournament was hosted by, and named after the great Bob Hope.

On day one Joel was paired with Swedish professional Henri Nolander and their amateur partners at the TPC Stadium Course. Nolander shot an uninspired two under par 70 and Dahmen shot an ugly 75 which left him in 141st place. For once, putting wasn't the main problem.

Bonnalie couldn't believe Dahmen's first driving range swing of the day. "He dropped his head and hit a week fade. This is a problem he had been working to correct for a couple of years and I thought he had it beaten. There was no trace of it in the practice rounds. But, here we were about to start the tournament and his old problem came back," Bonnalie moaned.

The problem stayed with him the next two days. In the second round at La Quinta, he got hot in the middle of the round and got it to six under with two holes to play. This put him back in position to challenge the cut line. He stepped to the 17th tee, moved the head and hit a week fade which led to a bogey. This was repeated on 18 and the bogey-bogey finished marred what could have been a good comeback. Even with the horrible finish, he passed a bunch of people with his 68 and stood 108th heading to round three at the Nicklaus course.

The head move continued and the resulting 72 left him at one under par and far short of the cut line. Once again, there was no check for either player or caddie and lack of money was getting to be a real issue.

Norlander ended up making $13,700 and Joel's old friend and competitor Nick Taylor cashed $28,700.

But the real surprise was Hadwin who Joel had beaten with ease on Tuesday. He shot a 59 in the second round, finished second in the tournament a cashed a check for $626,400!

***

The golf swing woe also exposed a building problem. Lack of caddie-player communication might be hindering Dahmen's performance.

When Joel agreed to hire Geno he made one rule. Under no circumstances was Bonnalie ever allowed to comment on his golf swing. This put Geno in a tough spot. He saw the head move immediately but had to keep his mouth shut and watch Joel self-destruct for three days. Bonnalie tried to tactfully address the touchy subject over a beer a day after the cut was missed but Dahmen remained steadfast. No commenting on golf swing mechanics was going to be allowed.

At this point, Geno decided on the indirect approach. He phoned Joel's swing coach Rob Rashell and outlined the problem. Rashell wrote Joel an e-mail and told him the same thing Geno was prepared to share several days earlier and Dahmen accepted the advice with great enthusiasm. "Think I'm fixed," he told Geno in an upbeat manner the following day.

***

The pattern of Joel struggling under pressure was becoming obvious and not surprising considering this was only his third start as a PGA rookie. He clearly blew check making opportunities in Mississippi and Georgia by three putting several holes in the clutch on the second day of both events. In La Quinta, the specific problem was different but the concern of not handling stress was the same. Almost all golfers have a negative swing tendency that can often show up under pressure. The very best players learn to manage this while the rest of us struggle.

All of this was an enigma because Dahmen's stated attitude seemed to be a perfect fit for the pressures of professional golf. He said in several interviews that "golf is what I do. It is my job but it is not who I am. I don't take my golf score home with me and let it dictate my happiness."

He went on to add "I know what a life and death is about and golf isn't it." This is a very true and certainly an understood and respected point of view from a cancer survivor who lost his mother to the disease in high school.

But, in a very real sense his stated attitude and actual performance seemed to be at odds with each other. Competing with the Tigers was clearly creating pressure.

As old pal Nick Taylor said "One weekend can change Joel's life but he's got to find a way to make it happen."

***

WINNER'S CIRCLE – Yet another first time PGA winner emerged and earned the benefits that go with tournament championships. These include the two-year exemption, invitations to the four majors and a million plus in cash.

This time it was 29 year-old Hudson Swafford who hoisted the trophy and he did it dramatic fashion by making birdies on holes 15 – 17 on Sunday afternoon for a one shot victory. This was especially impressive because famous architect Pete Dye claimed these were among the toughest holes he has ever designed.

Those closest to the PGA tour were not completely surprised by Swafford's performance. He had been playing well for quite a while and had made 19 consecutive cuts heading into the event.

CHAPTER TEN

JANUARY 30 AND February 2, 2017
SAN DIEGO, CA.

The disappointment in Palm Springs still lingered but there was no time to mope. Joel was still on the bubble for getting a place in the Farmer's Open Insurance tournament at the iconic Torrey Pines course in La Jolla, California which is a few miles north of San Diego. So he and Geno made the two-hour drive south to participate in the Monday qualifying event at El Camino Country Club.

Once again, the effort proved futile as his 72 wasn't close to earning a spot in the field. Mark Beker and Tyler Aldridge had fired 8 under par 64's and Michael McCabe and Brad Adamonis got in with rounds of 66.

Still, all was not lost as Joel got a call from a PGA official who said he was number one on the waiting list. This meant he and Geno would need to report to the course for Thursday's opening round and hope someone got injured or sick. They passed the time at the driving range trying to stay loose but the call never came for him to report to a tee so he was still hitting wedges as the day wore on. Finally, the driving range was empty except for Joel and the final threesome of the day current number two in the world Dustin Johnson, number one Jason Day and a guy named Tiger Woods. Joel might not have made the field but he was practicing next to golf royalty!

"So, when the three of them left the range, I grabbed our bag and Joel and I marched to the first tee like we belonged. I even grabbed a pin sheet from the starter table," Bonnalie smiled.

This was a great memory but once again, no check. Now, it was on to Phoenix for yet another draining and likely unproductive Monday qualifying event.

WALKING WITH TIGERS

***

Being on the driving range and warming up next to golf's biggest Tigers was a rarity for Joel and Geno. One might think this kind of thing happens often but actually interaction with the very top players is unusual for PGA rookies. Sometimes it seems like there are two tours – one for the "haves" and one for the "have-nots".

Rookies like Joel seldom see the more established players early in the week. Most tournaments have Wednesday Pro-Am events and the top players get in those and the rookies don't. Also, the established players tend to hang out together and play practices rounds with others like them. Rookies generally play their practice rounds with other rookies and players they know from mini tours or amateur competitions.

Veteran player and the central character of the book *BUD, SWEAT, & TEES* Rich Beem, described things this way. "As a rookie, when the tournament starts you're playing at such radically different times that by the time you are finished with your round those established guys have already gone home. If you do happen to be in the locker room or at the range at the same time, they're always surrounded by swing coaches and agents and manufacturers' reps and God knows who. It is a weird deal. You almost feel invisible sometimes."

CHAPTER ELEVEN

FEBRUARY 6, 2017
SCOTTSDALE, ARIZONA

One of the wildest and most popular PGA events is the Waste Management Phoenix Open held annually at the TPC of Scottsdale during super bowl week. It has a large and raucous gallery especially at the famous par three 16th hole where up to 30,000 fans cheer, hoot and boo tee shots while they are in the air. It is one of a kind! Joel had no chance of getting into this event unless he fired a near career round on Monday.

That didn't happen. He did manage a solid 65 but it took 63 at the rather easy McCormick Ranch qualifying site. Happily, the next event was the AT & T tournament in Monterey and Joel was guaranteed a spot in that field.

CHAPTER TWELVE

FEBRUARY 8 – 12
MONTEREY, CALIFORNIA

The rain was coming down so hard one could barely see 10 yards ahead and the wind was howling at near fifty knots when Geno Bonnalie arrived in beautiful Monterey, California and stepped foot on the iconic Pebble Beach course. It was Tuesday and the course was unplayable by any measurement. Still, Geno was "in heaven because this is Pebble" and he decided walking the course would be great fun. He even made a brief video that he shared with friends. It showed crashing ocean surf, flagsticks bending in half and rain coming down in buckets.

But Geno was smiling through it all and seemed happy as a clam. In one scene, he showed the one and only player on the entire course and said "I have a new favorite player. Look, Charlie Hoffman is actually practicing!"

***

Everyone who has played the crazy game of golf for any length of time is confounded by the potential highs and lows of a given round. A perfect example was Joel Dahmen's round one at the AT & T Pro Am Championship.

He had not been playing well in previous events and here he was in rainy, windy conditions on iconic Spyglass Hill, one of the sternest tests of golf on the PGA Tour. A tough round seemed to be a certainty because Spyglass can bring the World's best golfers to their knees even in perfect conditions.

"Joel came out and played like he did during his hot streak on the Web.com Tour last year. He wasn't doing anything special but he made his 6 – 12 foot putts and we were moving along nice and relaxed," said Bonnalie.

Dahmen had started on the 10th hole and standing on number 8 he was 5 under par with two holes to play. "Suddenly a cameraman appeared and it occurred to us that we must be somewhere around the lead. This thought seamed to unnerve Joel for a moment and he immediately 3 putted for bogey," Bonnalie recalled.

He then hit a perfect drive on the final hole but still had over 200 yards to the pin and a stiff wind was blowing right at him. He then hit what Bonnalie described as a shot that "went right of right." It ended up in a bush down by the snack shed and a rule official was called. A brief discussion led to a ruling of a free drop and Dahmen took advantage and hit a great shot to 15 feet, then dropped the putt for a miracle par.

The 68 was remarkable under the conditions and he was tied for the lead in a big-time PGA event! Interestingly, one of those tied with him was Rick Lamb whose caddie David Flynn was Geno's roommate for the week. "That night was pretty good. David and I went to Chilli's, had a snack and a couple of beers. We were two pumped up guys! Plus, my phone rang off the hook with messages of encouragement." Geno said.

***

The AT & T event was once known as the Crosby Clambake which was founded and hosted by the great singer and actor Bing Crosby, an avid golfer whose son Nathaniel was the US amateur champion in 1981 at the age of 19. Crosby and his dear friend Bob Hope hosted Pro-Am galas that attracted celebrities, sports figures, nationally known politicians and captains of industry. Their tournaments created tons of public interest and were largely responsible for the enormous golf boom of the 1940's. The event is unique because Bing set a format where all professionals had amateur partners and all teams played the first three days and the top 25 made it to Sunday's closing round. AT & T became the corporate sponsor in 1986 but kept the original format in honor of Crosby.

The clambake began in 1935 in San Diego and moved to Monterey in 1947. It is played on three courses and the cut is made at 54 holes rather than the traditional 36. The final round is always at Pebble Beach so the players who make the cut play there twice.

WALKING WITH TIGERS

Joel Dahmen's amateur partner was Willie Strothotte, one of the richest men in the world. Strothotte impressed Joel and Geno because he was "such a regular guy and was gracious to everyone."

This was Strothotte's 13th appearance in the event but it was only the second time he had made it to Sunday's round. The 72 year-old carries a 13 handicap and the team competition is net rather than best ball gross. During the four rounds, he contributed a whopping 23 strokes to the team total and this resulted in a tie for 12th place and put an additional $2500 in Joel's pocket.

***

Dahmen had an early tee time in Thursday's opening round so he was in the later block for round two at Pebble Beach on Friday. Rain delays meant he wouldn't be able to finish the round but the players were instructed to go as far as they could before play was suspended for darkness.

He started the day with a bogey on number one but got that stroke right back with a birdie on the second. Then he stayed calm and confident and made two more birdies and no bogeys before play was called due to darkness. He had completed 11 holes and stood at 6 under for the tournament. He was firmly near the top of the leaderboard and feeling good about his chances the next day.

***

It was cold when Dahmen and Bonnalie made their way to the long par three 12th hole at 7:30 to complete round two. Geno immediately sensed something was not right. "For whatever reason, things seemed different. He parred the 12th but bogeyed the easy 13th after a perfect drive left him 130 yards from the hole. A week iron and three putts followed and Joel was mad as hell," Geno said.

Another bogey was made at 16 and he scratched out shaky pars on 17 and 18. "The swing had left him and he wasn't nearly as confident as he was on the previous two days." Geno explained.

They were shuttled to Monterey Peninsula Country Club for round three. "We needed the break! Joel had a few minutes to hit balls and he quickly got his confidence back. He was ready to go again." Geno added.

Dahmen started the round at 4 under par, which despite giving away a couple of shots in the morning, still left him in great position. Things looked even better a few holes later as he played the first seven holes 3 under to get back on the front page of the tournament leaderboard at 7 under.

"It felt like old times. Geno and I were strolling around, joking a little and it was like we were back on the Web.com Tour," Joel recalled.

On the 8th, Dahmen's nemesis, the week push to the right, once again appeared. The ball ended up in a water hazard and Joel got hot at Geno for not warning him. But, in truth, Joel had himself to blame as the water should never have been an issue. Luckily, the ball was actually playable and Joel hit a spectacular recovery to within seven feet only to throw away the great recovery by three putting! He also three putted on the next hole but settled down and made a string of pars.

So, despite some woes he was still in great shape at five under par and firmly in tournament contention. Then the wheels came off once more.

He hit a week iron on the 16th hole and was 60 feet away from the cup. His first putt rolled 25 feet past and he had to make a five footer to save bogey. On the next hole he hit a week iron and chunked a chip for a double bogey and "it felt like a kick to the crotch. We went from high on the leaderboard to danger of missing the cut in the blink of an eye," Bonnalie noted.

The cut line became a non-issue when Dahmen scratched out a badly needed birdie on the last hole. This left him at 3 under heading into the final round back at Pebble Beach.

***

Sunday's final round was about survival and trying to cash a big a check as possible. Both player and caddie badly needed the money.

The round began on the difficult 10th hole. A good drive left a five iron to the green and before the shot Dahmen turned to Bonnalie and said "wow that water hazard is close." Sure enough the ball went into the hazard and the day started with double bogey.

A couple more bogeys followed and suddenly the first round co-leader was flirting with the bottom of the pack. Being totally out of contention seemed to settle Joel down and birdies on 17 and 18 plus a solid front nine added up to a 72 and a tie for 41st place. This earned a check of $17,897.

***

The highs and lows of this week are almost impossible to overstate. Leading a PGA event at a famous and challenging venue is very heady stuff. Plus, still being around the lead halfway through three rounds is very impressive. It should re-enforce the fact that Dahmen can play with the Tigers and he belongs on the PGA Tour. Plus, when all was said and done, he beat the likes of Stewart Cink, Phil Mickelson and Jim Furyk and cashed his first check in the big leagues.

Still, Joel and Geno can't help but think what might have been if only…

***

WINNER'S CIRCLE – Jordan Spieth built a six shot lead early in Sunday's final round and was never challenged en route to a four-shot win.

The twenty three year-old Texan won for the ninth time in his PGA career and became the first player since Tiger Woods with that many victories by age 24. Woods won 15 times. Equally impressive is he won for the fifth time by at least three strokes.

CHAPTER THIRTEEN

FEBRUARY 13
CITY OF INDUSTRY, CA.

Tired after four days of grinding hard at Pebble Beach, a weary Joel Dahmen made his way to the Los Angeles area and the first tee of the Industry Hills Golf Course. The goal was Monday qualifying for the popular Genesis Los Angeles Open held at the respected Riviera Country Club.

The odds of making the field via Monday qualifying is always a long shot especially the day after fighting tough weather and four six hour rounds at one of the toughest venues in all of golf.

Still, Joel put himself in a great position to qualify and was five under par after 17 holes. A birdie on the last would get him into the tournament and a par would earn him a spot in a playoff for the fourth and final spot in the field. The 18th at Industry Hills is a short par four and a perfect drive left him with a wedge to the pin. The birdie seemed very doable.

But, he hit a poor approach and then three putted. Once again, Joel's short game had left him at a critical moment and he was done for the week.

Kevin Tway and Jonathan Garrick shot 65 and 66 to claim the first two spots while Kevin Dougherty and JT Poston grabbed the final two positions with 67's.

CHAPTER FOURTEEN

MARCH 23 – 26, 2017
RIO GRANDE, PUERTO RICO

Los Angeles was the last stop on the west coast and the tour headed east to Florida and Texas. Joel Dahmen went to Scottsdale to practice and Geno Bonnalie went home to Lewiston to visit his family and earn some money by working for his dad.

The Honda Classic in Palm Beach, the World Golf championship in Mexico, the Valspar Championship in Palm Harbor, the Arnold Palmer Invitational in Orlando, and the World Golf Championship in Austin, Texas were all tournaments without openings for the lower ranking players.

The unwelcome rest stressed both player and caddie as the time passed with no competition or chance to improve their position. So, both Joel and Geno were raring to go and hoped good golf would be the story of their Puerto Rico trip to play in the Puerto Rican Open. Unfortunately, the main story ended up being about bugs – as in bed bugs and fire ants.

***

As usual, Geno was staying in a second-rate motel room with three other penny-pinching caddies. Meanwhile, Joel and Lona checked into the very nice looking tournament headquarters hotel. Yet it was Joel and Lona who ended up with the short stick on this particular room arrangement.

After two nights, both woke up covered with bed bug bites. "I had about 30 of them and they itched like crazy for the rest of the trip. I was okay after a couple of days but Lona had over 50 of them and they got big and sore. They still showed scarring a month later. She was really hurting and extremely uncomfortable," Dahmen said.

Geno's story was more dramatic and he described it this way:

"Thursday came and Joel played pretty solid. Nothing spectacular but a bogey free 69 was a decent start. We were in the last group on the second day and I knew the cut was going to be 3 or 4 under par. Joel made a couple of early bogeys and then on our fifth hole, our playing partner Nick Lindheim, snap hooked his tee shot into a hazard. He was unsure how to proceed so he asked for a rules official. As I started to walk away, I felt a burning sensation in my legs. I looked down and was covered in fire ants. I quickly brushed them away and took off my shoes but by then it was too late.

I had hundreds of bites. It was AWFUL! My shoes were filled with ants and I was not going to put them back on. I thought that trying to do my job would be the best way not to feel the pain. I went up and got Joel his yardage for his second shot and then again on his approach shot to the par five. As he was getting ready to hit his third shot, I knew something was very wrong. My thighs started to feel tight. I found a volunteer, took off my caddie bib and gave it to Lona, and I was taken to find a doctor at the nearby hotel. When I got to the hotel they wouldn't let me in because I wasn't a guest there so a nice lady ran in to find a doctor. I sat for about five minutes and my whole body began to break out in welts and hives. My skin was crawling. Everything from my toes up hurt. I felt like I was still being bitten and took my shirt off. As it turned out, I was just having a bad reaction to the bites.

My skin looked like cauliflower. I know how scary allergies can be and that people die from them all the time. That sure didn't calm me down and I was thinking I needed a hospital or, at the very least, get some Benadryl. I learned paramedics in Puerto Rico aren't allowed to give medicine. They didn't even have Benadryl. The doctor I eventually saw wrote me a prescription for a shot in the ass but I had to go to a pharmacy to get it! I was outraged! Someone just get me some fucking Benadryl! Someone drove me over to a parking lot and some nice people gave me ice but that wasn't helping anything.

The plan was for someone to drive to a pharmacy and get the medicine. From the time I got bit to the time the medicine arrived was only an hour but it seemed much longer. When the medicine did arrive, I yanked down my pants and the doctor shot me in the butt. I then popped two Benadryl and about 30 minutes later the swelling began to subside a little. By morning I was okay, but for a while I thought I was going to die in Puerto Rico."

***

While caddie Geno was fighting fire ants, Joel Dahmen, with girlfriend Lona Skutt on the bag, were trying to ignore the bed bug bites and play golf. He got in four more holes before nightfall and played them two under par. This left him at two under for the tournament with 10 holes left to play in the second round. The projected cut was minus four so it seemed he would have to play the last ten holes in two under to safely make the cut.

The next morning at 7 am and a shook, but willing, Geno back on the bag, Dahmen carded three birdies and two bogeys. Luckily, others had struggled also and the cut line rose to three under par which meant Joel made it by the skin of his teeth. The good news was this assured a needed paycheck.

Joel just didn't have it in round three and failed to make the secondary cut. He earned only $5370 but covered expenses because the bed bug bites and his firmness with hotel management resulted in four nights of free lodging. "Kind of a tough way to break even," Joel quipped.

***

WINNER'S CIRCLE – DA Points birdied his first five holes in Sunday's closing round and then hung on for a two-shot win over Bryson DeChambeau, Retief Goosen and Bill Lunde.

This was Points' third career victory on the PGA Tour and he was thrilled to have it. The title won't send him to the Master's because the tournament is played opposite a World Golf Championship but it still gives Points the important two-year exemption that goes with a tour victory. This was golden for Points because he had lost his card two years ago and had been struggling to get back on top.

CHAPTER FIFTEEN

March 27, 2016
CYPRESSWOODS COUNTRY CLUB
HOUSTON, TEXAS

How tough is it to Monday qualify for a PGA event? How about this. Six players shot eight under par 64's at the Cypresswoods Country Club and only one of them got into the tournament!

Joel Dahmen had left Puerto Rico and stopped in Houston to try to earn a spot in the Shell Houston Open. He shot a respectable 68 but it wasn't nearly good enough to win one of the coveted four positions left in the field.

Veteran PGA player Jason Gore was one of the six to card a 64 and he birdied the first playoff hole to garner the final place in the field. His playoff competitors were Roger Sloan, Brady Schnell, Martin Trainer, Sebastin Vazquez and Daniel Chopra.

Amateur and former mini tour player Riley Arp had earned medalist honors with a jaw dropping 62 and Andres Gonzalez and former University of Houston star Wes McClain had fired 63's to grab the second and third qualifying spots.

So, once again for Dahmen a Monday qualifying try had been fruitless but the success of Gonzalez showed the potential rewards. He finished 23rd and made $50,709. McClain made the cut and cashed $12,460.

Russell Henry won the Open and a whopping $1,260,000 prize while Dahmen's old buddy Nick Taylor cashed yet another check winning $21,750.

CHAPTER SIXTEEN

APRIL 20 – 21, 2016
SAN ANTONIO, TEXAS

The Shell event was the last tour stop before the Masters which was followed by the very popular RBC Heritage in beautiful Hilton Head, South Carolina. Theses tournaments were way out of reach for a PGA rookie so Joel Dahmen's next chance to compete was in the Valero Texas Open at AT&T Oaks in San Antonio.

Joel shook off a double bogey 6 on the 10th hole and scored a very respectable 2 under par 70 in Thursday's opening round. But a disastrous 41 on the front nine Friday doomed any chance of making the cut. He finished with 76 which left him at two over par. The cut ended up being even.

The event proved to be yet another disappointment for the Dahmen – Bonnalie duo but the end result provided further proof to what can happen if Joel could catch lightning in a bottle. Once again, the tournament championship was claimed by a first time winner.

***

WINNER'S CIRCLE - Kevin Chappell, making his 179th start on the PGA Tour, recorded his first victory and with it the $1,111,000 prize that went with the win. Two other first time winners Russell Henry at the Palmer event and Wesley Bryan at the RBC, had also became million dollar winners in recent weeks.

So, the dream of fame and fortune was very much alive, if not completely well, for the Joel – Geno team.

Also, Nick Taylor earned another nice check of $59,520 for finishing 22nd

while Nick Lindheim of the fire ant snap hook in Puerto Rico fame, made $42,160. This was yet further evidence that making some badly needed money could be close at hand. Joel knew he could beat any of these guys on any given day because he had done it.

***

Bonnalie's extreme cheapness on lodging arrangements was becoming legendary and source of amusement. Once again he ended up in a seedy motel but his time he had one roommate, Danny Renneisen who caddies for fellow PGA rookie Sebastin Munoz. They got to the hotel where the man who checked them in sat behind a steel cage because the neighborhood dictated the need for special safety measures.

They got their keys and went to the room where Geno noticed blood on his sheets. Danny thought that was funny until he pulled down the covers on his bed and saw even more blood. Not a good sign. Unhappy, the duo marched back down to the caged office, banged on the bars and issued their complaint. The man who checked them in sort of shrugged and said "wait a second" then grabbed a couple of new sheets, locked the office door behind him and changed the bedding himself.

Still, Geno was okay with this. "Hey, it was $130 for the whole week," he explained.

CHAPTER SEVENTEEN

MAY 4 AND 5
WILMINGTON, NORTH CAROLINA

Joel Dahmen tells the story of how he became fully aware of the perils of being a caddie and it comes as no surprise that Geno Bonnalie was part of the tale.

The pair had entered a two-man best ball tournament held in Scottsdale during the weekend of the Masters. In the second and final round, they were playing well and were in contention to win a nice amount of prize money. Joel was having a tough hole on the back nine so it was up to Geno to carry them and keep the momentum going.

Bonnalie's drive on the par four was in fair position. It was barely in the rough and the lie was not a bad one. Geno was ready to hit a low shot under a tree and run the ball to the front of the green where he could likely two putt and save par. But, Joel came over and, after a lengthy discussion, talked Geno's into hitting a lob wedge over the tree.

"Geno wasn't comfortable with that choice and sure enough he chunked the shot, hit the tree, and we walked away with bogey. He was pissed at me and I couldn't blame him. I NOW have total sympathy in what it is like to walk in his shoes," Joel laughed.

***

The "Lewiston Flightmare", the travel schedule Bonnalie faces on almost every road trip, was never more in view than the journey to meet Dahmen in Wilmington, North Carolina for the Wells Fargo Championship.

Geno left Lewiston a 7:30 am on Saturday, April 29h and made the two hour drive to Spokane where he had found a cheap though complicated fare to the tournament site. He left Spokane around noon and flew to Phoenix, then Indianapolis then Charlotte and finally Raleigh where he rented a car and made the two hour drive to Wilmington. This took 25 hours and Geno, who has great difficulty sleeping on planes, was exhausted when he arrived.

To make matters worse, the week's lodging arrangement was a KOA campsite, in a tent with three other caddies. The glamour of being on the PGA Tour and living in first class facilities seemed very far away indeed.

Still, the always optimistic Geno said "hey, the tent was fun the first couple of nights. Then this big storm hit but luckily Joel and Lona invited me to stay with them that night."

***

The tournament was held at the Eagle Point Golf Club, which according to Bonnalie, "was the nicest golf course I have ever seen. Two of my tent mates have caddied at the Masters and both said the Eagle Point facility is as close to Augusta National as it gets in terms of being pristine and in perfect condition."

Unfortunately, Joel's game didn't measure up to the conditions and the long, tiresome trip ended with another missed cut and another week without a check. Once again, the short game was the culprit as the frustration kept building for player and caddie alike.

Dahmen opened with an embarrassing 80 and said "I didn't get the ball up and down once during the entire round. It was bad." He followed that up with an uninspired 74 and beat only five players in the entire field of 156.

After putting out on the final hole of the opening round, Dahmen broke his putter in half and had to borrow one for round two. "He needs more than a new putter, he needs a radical change. Maybe go cross handed or try a long putter or whatever. He is in a major putting funk," said Bonnalie.

As is often the case, Joel had played a pre tournament practice round with Nick Taylor and "had held his own," Geno observed. But when the lights went on and the actual tournament started, it was a whole different story. Taylor finished 8th and won $210,000. Joel and Geno went home.

***

WINNER'S CIRCLE - Brian Harman made a dramatic birdie with a 28-foot putt on the final hole to win the event. He knew a birdie was needed to avoid a playoff with Dustin Johnson and Pat Perez and he delivered. The 18th is a par five and Harman's second shot went a bit long and landed in some deep grass which left him with a very difficult chip. He semi chunked the chip but then stepped up and drained the putt which set off a joyous celebration with caddie Scott Tway and the Harman family.

The big birdie denied Johnson a chance at a piece of golf history. Johnson, who was now number one in the world rankings, was trying for his fourth straight victory a feat unheard of in modern day PGA golf.

This was Harman's second appearance in the PGA winner's circle. He won the John Deere Classic in 2014.

Geno, Danica Patrick & Joel

Dustin Johnson

Young Holly

Caddie's Motel Room

Geno's Guinness Run

Geno in Competition

Geno the young archer

Young Geno

Geno & niece, Tina Flerchinger Cystinosis Fund Raiser

The Bonnalies

Halloween with the Bonnalies

Geno & Holly

Official Caddy Card

Holly's birthday tweet

Genomobile

Joel's trophies

Young Lona

Joel, Zach, Ed & Jolyn

Joel & Lona

Joel, Lona & Friend

Joel with Bob & Leinani Yosaitis

Young Joel

Coveted PGA Card

Joel the Professional

Waffle House Guys

King of the Hill

Buddy Nick Taylor

CHAPTER EIGHTEEN

MAY 18 – 21, 2017
IRVING, TEXAS

From Wilmington, the tour's top players went to the Players Championship at the TPC Sawgrass in Ponte Vedra Beach, Florida. The event is just a notch below the four majors in prestige and the field is always among the strongest of the PGA season. This meant Joel Dahmen and Geno Bonnalie had another week off prior to the AT&T Byron Nelson at the Four Season's Resort in Irving, a Dallas suburb.

During the break Joel made physical changes during practice sessions. He changed his ball position slightly by moving it back in his stance. He also changed putters and his putting grip. Essentially, he went to the "claw" which is a grip where two fingers of the right hand are on the putter shaft. This tends to lessen the influence of the right hand during the putting stroke.

Getting to Dallas was easy for Joel consisting of the usual non-stop flight from Phoenix and even Geno had it good avoiding the "Lewiston Flightmare" by catching a one-stop flight directly from Lewiston.

Once again, Geno was sharing a room with Danny Renneisen who works for Sebastin Munoz. They were staying less than a mile from the course so they saved additional money by walking to the course and avoiding the cost of a rental car. Plus, there were no bloody sheets or caged registration desks.

Coincidently, Munoz, a 24-year-old rookie with $303,000 in earnings, was one of the players paired with Dahmen in the first two rounds. The other was Tyler Aldridge, an Idahoan with $880,000 in career money.

***

The Four Season's course is a pretty narrow par 70 made more challenging than usual during round one because of 25 mile per hour winds. Dahmen hit his opening tee shot in a fairway bunker and started his round with a bogey five before settling down to shoot a very handy two under par 68. This left him in a tie for 14th four shots behind leader James Hahn. Munoz had fired a 69 but Aldridge struggled with a 77.

The key to the solid round was the par five sixteenth. The hole was playing dead into the wind and there was no chance to reach it in two shots. Joel laid up nicely and then hit "a perfect" wedge that should have left him a tap in for birdie. Unfortunately, the shot hit the flagstick and boomeranged a full 30 feet away. This was a terrible piece of bad luck but Joel took it in stride and calmly knocked in the putt for birdie. "He could have let that break get to him but he didn't. He balled up and drained the putt! That was a huge turnaround," Bonnalie said proudly. The 68 tied notables Jordan Spieth and Jason Day and was one better than Nick Taylor. Also, the new putting grip was working like a charm. Joel had played a competitive round without a three putt.

***

The second round was played under ideal conditions and Jason Kokrak roared to the head of the pack by firing an impressive 62 for a two-day total of 10 under par.

Joel started on the tenth hole and pulled his drive slightly. But, he hit a spectator and the ball ended up in perfect position in the fairway. Walking from the tee Dahmen turned to Bonnalie and said "what do I do? I don't have anything to give the guy. We don't have any spare gloves or balls and I sure don't have any money." So, Joel walked over to the man who was about 50 and apologized for not having anything to give him.

Dahmen went about his business and hit his second shot to within 6' and made the putt for birdie. Then he began to feel bad and sent Geno back to get the man's phone number so he could get something to him later. The man said "great, I'll take a dozen balls." Geno thought this was "a hair on the pushy side."

Both Joel and Geno forgot about the incident though they would have remembered and done something later because they are thoughtful people. But, after the round the brazen man was waiting for them at the scorer's table and said, "I'll take my dozen balls now."

***

Joel parred the next five holes and then got some Golf Channel television time by almost holing his tee shot on the par three seventeenth. He tapped in for birdie and followed up with a 20-foot putt for another birdie on the 18th. This put him at 5 under par for the tournament and firmly on the front page of the leaderboard.

He still had to play the front nine and he didn't fare nearly as well. He made bogeys on three of the final four holes. His 36-hole score was two under which left him tied for 25th place but well inside the cut line of two over par. Sebastin Munoz was also at two under par after shooting another 69.

***

The back nine had not been kind to Joel Dahmen so far in his rookie year but this changed in Saturday's third round. He bogeyed the second hole and then strung together 10 solid pars before heading to the par three thirteenth. He knocked his tee shot to ten feet and drained the putt to get back to even for the day and still two under for the tournament. This birdie boosted his confidence and he was determined to finish strong. He did just that.

He hit a wedge to three feet on the par five sixteenth and converted the putt for birdie. He duplicated that feat with another beautiful wedge and tap-in on 18. The finish put Joel at four under par for the tournament which left him in a tie for 24th heading to Sunday's final round.

***

The moment of truth had arrived. Young Joel and his trusty friend and caddie Geno Bonnalie had just earned the right to walk with the biggest Tiger on the face of the planet! Joel Dahmen, PGA rookie from small town America, was in a 10:55 am twosome with none other than Dustin Johnson, the World's number one ranked player.

To list Johnson's credentials would take a book of its own. Currently, he is number one in the world ranking and is also number one in Fed Ex points and money earned in 2017. To date, he has won over $6,000,000, a full $2 million more than the closest competitor. He is also an intimidating physical specimen who hits drives of legendary proportions and is number one on the tour in driving distance.

Playing with Johnson in 2017 is like being paired with Tiger Woods or Jack Nicklaus at the height of their careers. The gallery following them was going to be huge and raucous.

The round was going to be quite a test for young Dahmen who had never been paired with a top fifty player before. In addition, national television coverage was almost a certainty which added to the hoopla.

The rookie learning curved had just spiked up. Way up.

***

A heavy thunderstorm delayed the start of play on Sunday morning so the PGA made a decision to revise the schedule and play the final round in groups of three. After the change, Dahmen was still paired with Johnson but now Kevin Tway was also with them. This gave Joel a bit of tummy comfort because he had played with Tway often including a practice round on Tuesday.

In addition, he was a symbol of how things could be for Joel if he got his own game in order. Tway had played on the PGA Tour in 2014 but lost his card for a year and, like Joel, got it back based on Web.com standings in 2016. Tway was taking full advantage of his second try and has won a nifty $1,200,000 so far in 2017. More importantly, he is in the top sixty in Fed Ex points and seems a cinch to retain his playing card for 2018.

The downside of Tway's involvement was Joel was going to have to avoid the natural urge to get into a distance contest with his playing partners. On average, Tway is only seven yards shorter off the tee than Johnson so Dahmen was paired with a couple of guys who are monsters when it comes to driving the golf ball.

Joel and Geno arrived at the course at their normal time and went through their regular practice routine in preparation for the round. "Actually, I was doing a pretty good job of keeping my nerves in check until I made my way to the tee. Right off the bat I knew things were very, very different. This guy about 6'5" and 300 pounds introduced himself saying he was Dustin's personal bodyguard. Then the PGA Tour head of security showed up and finally, four police officers arrived. We had never needed security before. Then I looked down the fairway where I usually see about ten people. This time there were hundreds," Joel laughed.

"Still I was holding up okay when I met Dustin and shook hands with Kevin. Then, after a few minutes of fog, they called my name and the nerves hit me like waves. This is really happening. I've got to go hit a shot," he added.

Joel responded to the challenge like a veteran. He piped his first drive right in the middle of the fairway and went on to make routine two-putt pars on the first two holes. "This solid start helped calm Joel a bit and you could see him beginning to focus. Also, I cannot overstate how much Dustin Johnson helped. He talked with us all the way down the first fairway and treated us like peers. He could not have been more gracious. He knew what we were experiencing and he was going out of his way to help," Bonnalie said.

At one point early in the round Dustin and Geno were alone for a couple of minutes and Johnson asked how many starts Joel had gotten to date. Geno responded that this was only their eight and Dustin said "wow that is tough. I'm rooting for you guys." "And, he did. I didn't know what to expect but I am a big Dustin Johnson fan now," Geno said.

**

Joel was working hard to keep his nerves in check. Meanwhile, Geno was having a ball. "The excitement, the buzz and the adrenaline were giving me a rush! This is exactly why I want to be out here," Geno said.

Girlfriend Lona Skutt was trying to watch the action but the size of the gallery made it difficult. "Usually there about 10 people watching Joel play so following him is a nice leisurely walk. Not today! I had to rush ahead and then crowd around the greens as best I could. It was a madhouse. Everyone wants to see Dustin Johnson hit drives so the tees were stacked with people ten rows deep. But, it was exciting and I was having fun," Lona said.

***

Golfers know that in every round there are moments of truth and how they are handled is almost always the key to the success or failure of a round. On this day, Joel Dahmen's first such encounter happened on the par four third hole, statistically the hardest hole on the course. He knocked his second shot in a greenside bunker and hit a decent sand shot that left him a curling, side hill seven-footer to save par. He made the putt and that seemed to ignite him in a big way.

He carded a routine par on the 4th and then got red hot and made three birdies in a row. On the par three 5th hole he hit a solid iron to ten feet and dropped the putt.

Then on six he got a good break when his tee shot hit the cart path and ended up 366 yards off the tee in perfect position. From there he hit a wedge to 14" and tapped in.

He capped the streak on the par five seventh. His drive was in the trees but he hit a perfect low iron that left him with a good angle to the pin for his third shot. His wedge ended up four feet away and he dropped that putt also. Suddenly, Dahmen was seven under par and on the front page of the leaderboard.

***

Joel's first ever face-to-face encounter with a top fifty player was going unbelievably well but Dustin Johnson was struggling with his game and was one over par through seven holes. Despite this, on every hole gallery members were screaming things like - "hey, DJ will you sign my hat, or yelling for 400-yard shots to go in the hole or other really dumb stuff. They were unbelievably obnoxious. They didn't ever leave him alone," Bonnalie said.

Joel asked Johnson if it was like this all the time and did he ever get tired of this kind of attention. "Yeah, it is always pretty much like this and it can get old at times. But, I can't make this kind of money any other way so I have learned to put up with it,' Johnson smiled. "Plus, most people are out here to have fun and very few ever cause trouble."

Lona Skutt agreed. "Actually, the people were great. Sometimes they were loud and silly but everyone was good natured."

***

Joel was playing beautiful golf in the PGA pressure cooker and was three under par through seven holes. Now he needed to keep it together and that was not going to be easy. The pressure was increasing and the nerves were ramping back up as he got further into the round. The crowds were also getting even bigger and rowdier and, now that Joel was on the leaderboard, some gallery members were asking him for autographs and high fives too.

Nevertheless, Joel was doing a great job of saying focused. The claw grip was working and he kept making solid chips and putts resulting in pars on the eighth, ninth and tenth holes.

***

On the eleventh hole a couple of things happened. Direct TV via a linkup with ESPN picked up live coverage of the threesome on its featured group telecast with former PGA player Billy Kratzert hosting the action. Viewers got to see nearly every shot Dahmen, Johnson and Tway hit the rest of the way.

Second, Lona was noticed by security and ushered inside the ropes. She now had a front row view and even got high fives from gallery members who figured "I must be somebody."

***

On number eleven Joel hit a perfect drive and a wedge to eleven feet. He knocked that putt dead center and suddenly he was four under par for the day and eight under for the tournament. He was tied for fourth! "Now the adrenaline was really flowing and Geno and I were trying very hard to keep that in mind when we were picking clubs," Joel said.

Kratzert spoke of the importance of the round for Joel and noted that he was a cancer survivor and for the first, but certainly not the last time, praised his poise.

Johnson also birdied and Tway salvaged a par.

***

Number twelve is the second hardest hole on the course and after a perfect drive Dahmen faced another moment of truth. Bonnalie described the hole this way. "We were a bit between clubs. We had about 185 to the hole which is a usual practice range six iron. But, the wind seemed to be directly at us and we agreed a comfortable five iron was the right choice. Then Joel hit his best looking shot of the day! It was all over the flag and though we couldn't see the pin from our angle, I knew we had another birdie! But, then there was dead silence from the gallery and we looked at each other and shook our heads. What's wrong?"

Joel said "we walked up there and saw the ball. It had gone long and it couldn't have been in a worse spot. I was short-sided, having no green to work with and the lie was terrible. Plus, I was in deep grass. The shot I thought was perfect in the air ended up being a disaster."

Dahmen decided to try a very risky chip shot. He hooded (closed the face) on a nine iron and decided to bump the ball into the hillside and hoped for a favorable bounce that would put him somewhere on the green. He hit the shot as planned and got a very good bounce leaving him eight feet from the hole. "Luckily, we got a good read from Kevin who was on a similar line and Joel knocked his putt in the middle of the cup for a remarkable par," Bonnalie said.

In the booth, Kratzert raved about the chip and gave it an 8.5 out of 10. Geno said, "It was a lot better than that!"

Johnson and Tway both bogeyed the hole.

***

On thirteen, Joel was still a bit excited about the saved par on twelve and "hit a shaky tee shot," to a greenside bunker. His sand shot was mediocre and left him with a 12' putt. He missed that one but Kratzert said he liked the putting stroke and complimented Joel's calm demeanor. Now it was once again a matter of holding it together for the finishing holes to secure a much needed check and coveted FedEx Cup points.

Tway made a birdie and Johnson a par.

On the fourteenth tee the announcers said they were anxious to see how Joel would react to his first bogie. Skutt was also worried saying to herself "hang in there Joel I want to pay off our credit cards."

At the same time Joel turned to Geno and said with a smile "I'm so nervous I think I'm going to puke." At which point Geno replied "Nah, not nervous this is fun! Like the old days."

Nerves or no, Joel responded with a perfect tee shot and had 110 yards left to a "green light pin" Perhaps adrenaline influenced this shot too because Joel hit it dead at the pin but almost 50' too long. But, once more Joel responded to the challenged and hit a beautiful lag putt to two feet and then tapped it in to save par.

Johnson hit his second shot close and made birdie but Tway drove it in the rough and ended up with a bogey.

***

"Now I was the most nervous I had been all day. I wanted to finish without a stumble and I was grinding hard to stay focused," Joel said.

His drive on fifteen was perfect in the right center of the fairway and he followed that with a great looking iron that took an extra big hop and bounced over the green. The announcers termed it a "terrible break" and once again Joel, with the pressure way up, was looking at an extremely difficult and touchy chip shot.

Joel and Geno weighed the options and then Joel lobbed a picture perfect wedge to tap in range for another clutch par. "This kid has talent! That was awesome especially under the circumstances!" Kratzert cried. "What nerves!" he added.

Tway made a routine par and Johnson drove it in the trees and took a bogey.

***

All three players hit solid tees shots on the par five sixteenth hole and all had chances of hitting the green in two shots. Dahmen and Tway missed the green to the right while Johnson, 25 yards in front of Joel, knocked an iron in the middle of the green.

Between shots, the announcers analyzed all three of the player's swings using slow motion and stop action tools and they called Dahmen's swing "text book". Also, the cheers for Joel were ramping up and the gallery was giving him big-time encouragement.

An excited Kratzert said "Dahmen executed that shot to perfection. That is three fabulous up and downs on this side! His frame of mind is tremendous."

Dahmen tapped in his putt for birdie and Johnson and Tway had pars.

***

Lona tries not to look at scoreboards during a round but she couldn't help it after the birdie on sixteen because there was a huge board right in front of her. The board showed the position. Her beloved Joel was eight under par and tied for fourth!

"Things were streaking through my mind. Nervous doesn't begin to describe how I felt. Smiles, joy, tears, relief, dread, all at the same time," she gushed.

She was shown on the Direct TV coverage and was incorrectly called Joel Dahmen's wife. Later this was corrected. Asked how long they had been married, Lona replied "we aren't married yet but this might help," which brought good-natured chuckles from the announcing crew.

Now those at home without Direct TV would be a part of the action as the national CBS television coverage followed Joel on his final two holes. During that, the play-by-play announcers commented on how tough things had gone during Dahmen's rookie season and they also shared with the national audience that he was a cancer survivor.

On the par 3 seventeenth Joel stepped on the tee and surveyed the scene. He turned to Dustin Johnson and said "DJ, what is your resting heart rate?" Dustin answered "I don't know, why?" "You don't look like you even have a pulse and my heart is beating so hard I'm afraid it's going to come out of my chest," Dahmen joked. Johnson got a good chuckle and seemed to further admire how Joel was dealing with madness surrounding the group.

Nerves and adrenaline were flowing in flood-like proportions but Joel hit a beautiful seven iron right over the pin about twenty feet from the cup. The putt was a slick downhiller and Joel didn't make things easy on himself when he ran it three to four feet past. On television, the putt seemed easy but it wasn't, especially under the circumstances. Joel had struggled with his putter and all season and now he had to make this one in front of a huge gallery, for major money, on national television. Hands and knees were knocking but he made it and breathed a huge sigh of relief. Bonnalie said "I was barely able to breath and when he made it I literally got goose bumps."

Johnson and Tway also got pars.

***

Dahmen was still three under par for the day going to the final hole. The CBS announcers explained his situation and how badly he needed the money and FedEx points. There was still one hole to go and every stroke was critical.

Joel's tee shot on eighteen was dead straight right at his intended target. But, adrenaline and luck worked against him and the ball rolled into a fairway bunker. Had it gone a few inches less it would have been perfect. Even a few inches more would have been okay as it would have left him with a straight forward bunker shot of about a hundred yards. As it turned out, the ball was barely in the trap and Joel had to stand outside the trap and try to gouge it somewhere around the green. Johnson walked over and took a look and said "wow, what a crappy break."

Joel hit a respectable shot but it was a bit thin and the ball flew over the green leaving him a terribly difficult pitch to a downhill pin. The challenge of the round was far from over because leaving the chip short or blading it over the green were very real possibilities and either mishit could lead to double bogey or worse. But once again Joel responded to the intense pressure and hit a chip to about 20 feet. He missed the putt and made bogey but kept the beautiful round intact by shooting a solid 67. Johnson had carded a 69 and finished in a tie for 13th while Tway shot 71 and ended up tied for 20th.

***

WINNER'S CIRCLE - Billy Horschel won the tournament when Jason Day, the second ranked player in the World, three-putted the first hole of a playoff. Ironically it was Day's only three putt of the entire week.

This was Horschel's first win in almost three years and his fourth PGA title. It jumped him from 71st to 15th in the FedEx Cup standings and his strong performance was certainly no surprise to those close to the PGA Tour. Horschel has won over $15,000,000 in his career and won the 2014 FedEx playoff.

FINAL LEADERBOARD
Billy Horschel -12 $1,350,000
Jason Day -12 810,000
James Hahn -11 510,000
Jason Kokrak -10 360,000
Danny Lee -8 263,000
Sean O'Hair -8 263,000
Byeong Hun An -8 263,000
Bud Cauley -8 263,000
Joel Dahmen -7 195,000
Matt Kucher -7 195,000
Nick Taylor -7 195,000
Cameron Triagale -7 195,000

***

Joel Dahmen had beaten the best player in the World head-to-head on a Sunday afternoon. He had tied for ninth with Matt Kucher, Cameron Triagale and old friend Nick Taylor who had lit up the weekend scoreboard with rounds of 65 and 66. In the process, he had moved from 221st to 173rd in the Fed Ex cup standings. His day had gone far above expectations and, at least for now, he had exorcised some very bad demons.

Plus, the check won was $195,000. This was a huge thing for player and caddie alike because they had only earned $28,000 in all of the previous 2017 events combined.

In a television interview after the round Dahmen once again showed great poise and handled himself like a veteran. He thanked Nick Taylor for his help with logistics saying "Everything is new out here and Nick has been great helping me adjust." Meanwhile, Taylor warmly congratulated Joel for his great day during his own post round interview.

Geno Bonnalie was beaming and smiling ear-to-ear. Several people had come up to him and said kind and generous things. His phone was full of congratulations and positive messages.

Lona Skutt couldn't stop smiling.

The three deserved this moment of joy because the season had been a rough one. Would this impressive finish serve as a springboard and vault Dahmen to more high points for the rest of the season? Time would tell that tale.

CHAPTER NINETEEN
HALFWAY

The Byron Nelson tournament marked the halfway point of the 2016 – 17 regular season schedule for Joel Dahmen and Geno Bonnalie. They will get to play in seven of the remaining PGA events with no Monday qualifying or stress of being on a waiting list.

This gives them eight more chances to keep their playing card for 2017 - 2018. The criteria has been simplified a bit and basically the easiest path is this: the top 125 in Fed Ex Cup points get full PGA playing status while those ranked 125 – 200 will have a chance to retain their cards only if they succeed in the season-ending Web.com Tour playoffs.

Dahmen had earned 75 points for his finish in the Nelson and now sat in the 173rd position with 82 points. Currently the number 125th ranked player is Shane Lowry with 204 points.

Ironically, the money and FedEx Cup points for a top ten finish in the Nelson didn't add to Joel's tournament opportunities. He would have gotten in these less popular tour events even if he had still been ranked 221st in the FedEx pecking order. Had a top ten finish happened in one of the early tournaments, the corresponding rise in status would have gotten him in two to four more starts.

Still, no friend or family members were complaining about the Byron Nelson finish. Not by a long shot!

If nothing else the financial pressure was now off Dahmen because Lona was able to pay off current bills and charge cards and there was enough money in the bank to cover travel expenses for the rest of the season.

The Bonnalies, due to Holly's good job and Geno's thriftiness on the road, had been holding their own financially. Now they had a few extra dollars in their coffers and things were looking up.

Also, the finish was a big-time affirmation to Joel's confidence. He had looked the number one player in the eye and had more than held his own. He had faced the most pressure of his golf career and performed brilliantly. "We felt like we had won the tournament and we couldn't stop smiling," Lona said.

Geno put it even more distinctly "We kicked'butt!"

All were hoping the good Nelson showing would serve as a springboard to solid play and create more top ten finishes in the season's final events. Dahmen and Bonnalie would drop back down to the Web.com Tour next year if they had to, but they sure weren't looking forward to that possibility.

Everything about the PGA experience is superior. As an example, the money Joel made for finishing in a tie for ninth at the Nelson was more than two FIRST PLACE checks on the Web.com. Plus, the venues, the hospitality, the host hotels, the courtesy cars and other perks are all significantly better than anything the smaller tour can provide. Also, players and caddies get first rate free food at all of the PGA tournament sites which adds up to a huge cost savings during the course of a season.

Losing PGA playing privileges would be a disappointment. Nevertheless, reality and history shows that only a handful of the 2016 Web.com class will still be around next season. Joel and Geno hoped to be on the elite list but a lot of work needed to be done to accomplish that.

Basically, the future would begin to focus more clearly in July when Dahmen played in five events in consecutive weeks.

***

The outlook was hopeful for the remainder of the year but the low points were not forgotten. The broken hand had started things off in the worst possible way and cost Dahmen the chance to move up the priority chart. This turned out to be a big deal because even a small upwards move early on would have given him more tournament entries.

Then, when he did get a chance to play, he was nagged by three-putts, back nine collapses and missed cuts. Meanwhile, the travel expenses were adding up and every opportunity to play was overloaded with pressure to cash a check.

There were down times for sure. Geno Bonnalie was often lonely because Lona was traveling with Joel full-time and Geno was often by himself in strange towns. He talked to wife Holly every night but missed hanging out with his son, Hudson.

The "Lewiston Flightmare" – hard, inconvenient travel - contributed to this. Geno's lowest points were often his flights and car rides home after missed cuts because he had time to fret about the long breaks between tournament opportunities.

There are also insensitive people to face when he gets home. Geno and Holly are very protective of Joel and they hate it when people make negative remarks about his struggles on the golf course. They tire of remarks like "what are you going to do next year" or "why does he three-putt all the time," etc.

Privately, the Bonnalies were also worried that Joel would look for another caddie to help guide him out of the slump. There was never any indication that Joel was considering this but Holly felt the possibility existed. "Financially, firing wouldn't hurt but this is still Geno's dream and I want him to keep going for it," she said firmly.

***

The first part of the season was also very hard on Lona Skutt who is a self-proclaimed "worry wart" by nature. "I have complete confidence in Joel and know he will succeed but watching him struggle is so hard! When someone you love hurts, so do you. There are times when the disappointment is overwhelming and we have had some good cries," she shared.

Lona has traveled with Joel to every tournament this year and has walked with him in almost every round. She said the hardest part is watching and not being able to do anything to help. Also, there have been times when she feels guilty about quitting her job and not contributing to the household income. "Joel always calms me down and talks me out of that. He says he wants me out there with him and he is good about assuring me things will be okay. But, I'm old-fashioned and practical and not being able to pay off my credit card every month bothers me sometimes," she adds.

The worst time for Lona was during a one day US Open qualifying tournament in Tucson in early May. That day, he was bombing his drives and hitting great looking irons. "The normal Joel Dahmen would have taken advantage of those shots and been a whole bunch under par. This Joel Dahmen three-putted almost every hole and I saw a look on his face I had never seen before. He was an utterly and totally beaten man. He had fear in his eyes," Lona remembered.

Joel told Lona he had the yips and wanted to leave the course with five holes to play. She talked him into finishing the round but it had not been a good day for them.

***

Others were feeling the effects of the bad play but it was Joel Dahmen himself who carried the biggest burden. Only he could change things and he was beginning to have doubts about his ability to play with the Tigers. He had never experienced this much concern about his golf game and he was worried. "Geno was telling me things would work out. My coach told me I was close. Friends and family told me to be patient. But, hey, this was getting to me," he related.

Joel had always been good about not letting a bad day on the golf course get to him. His experience with cancer had taught him what was important in life and he usually kept the game in its rightful perspective. But, this slump was different. The hardest part was he felt he was letting everyone down. Plus, the time off between tournaments was preventing him from getting any momentum. The massive flame outs in San Antonio and Wilmington were "like a kick in the balls."

Still, Dahmen is not the type of person to give up and the continued success of Nick Taylor was a positive sign things could improve at any time. Also, a few members of his Web.com class of 2016 were doing well and were in a good position to keep their playing cards for next season. Those who were in the top 125 going into Memorial Day were:

PLAYER FEDEX RANK & POINTS MONEY WON
McKenzie Hughes 18/852 1,876,828
Wesley Bryan 19/850 2,005,835

Ollie Schniederjans 45/527 1,179,264
Kelly Kraft 50/502 1,205,227
Kevin Tway 59/462 1,097,225
C.T. Pan 81/397 883,578
Dominic Bozzelli 96/420 675,301
J.T. Poston 97/296 573,131
Ryan Blaum 110/281 539,602
Michael Thompson 113/268 500,873
Scott Stallings 120/248 455,026

Joel had found a way to feel positive when he had stepped to the tee with Dustin Johnson at the Nelson. Would that finish and the resulting confidence propel him to a hot second half?

CHAPTER TWENTY

MAY 23 – 25
SCOTTSDALE, ARIZONA

PGA professionals seldom play in local tournaments but the Scottsdale Open was being held at Talking Stick, a club 10 minutes from Joel Dahmen's house. He also was feeling good about his game and was anxious to get back on the course. So, he decided to be a last minute entry and play in the event.

It proved to be a profitable decision as he shot rounds of 68-64-68 and cruised to an easy victory. This was a nice affirmation that his game was in a good place and the $20,000 winner's prize further padded the checkbook. The claw grip and slight change in ball position were helping a lot.

Young Joel was now in a different mindset and could hardly wait to play in his next PGA event.

CHAPTER TWENTY-ONE

LEWISTON, IDAHO
MAY 26 – 29

One of the most popular golf tournaments in the Lewis-Clark Valley is the LT Classic a 54 hole, two-man event held at the Lewiston Country Club on Memorial Day weekend.

Geno Bonnalie had entered the event with friend Corey Brown, a 40 year-old who had grown up in the area and had won many local tournaments over a twenty-five year golfing career. Brown is a scratch player and he and Bonnalie were among the pre-tournament favorites to win the low gross title.

Geno was treated like a celebrity after the success of the Nelson tournament and was in high spirits going into the weekend. He was happy to be with his many friends and was looking forward to enjoying some great golf and participating in the social events that are a major part of the LT Classic. But, sometimes things just don't work out.

Saturday's opening round was fine and Geno and Corey were in contention after day one. Saturday evening's Calcutta is always a good time and Geno and Holly Bonnalie were able to have a pleasant evening of fellowship with friends.

Sunday started okay but then went downhill quickly. Geno's game was rusty and "I flat assed stunk," he said. Brown was also playing poorly and broke his big toe when he kicked his golf cart after a wayward shot. His playing companions showed great sympathy of course and insisted on authorizing the toe by signing it with a red Sharpie.

Geno and Corey decided that a few adult beverages after the round would get them in prime condition for the final round on Monday. That strategy didn't work but it did result in fully clothed dips in the swimming pool and seats in Holly's doghouse.

Interestingly enough, the pair drew tournament co-host Joe Strohmaier and Chris Thomas as their playing companions for Monday's closing round. Thomas happens to be Joel Dahmen's contact at Cool Clubs Golf in Scottsdale and he spoke glowingly about Joel. "Joel has the perfect attitude and I think he has the talent and outlook to make it big. Some guys come to us with a know-it-all mentality and end up gaining nothing from us. Not Joel. I really like him," Thomas said.

Golfing results for the Bonnalie – Brown team? "Don't ask." groaned Geno.

CHAPTER TWENTY-TWO

JUNE 5 – 11
MEMPHIS, TENNESSEE

Geno Bonnalie was out of wife Holly's doghouse and she set a goal for him for the season's second half - Try to get home with your own clothes.

"These guys have as many as four to a room on occasion and, sometimes when I help Geno unpack, we find strange underpants, socks, etc. Once I found a pair of shorts that looked like they belonged to Big Al or something. They were huge," Holly said. "But, this also gives me a chance to have a little fun. One time I yelled 'Hey Geno, what is this condom doing in your suitcase?' There was no condom of course but it felt good to pull his chain. Geno was not as amused as I was but I was having a good time," she added.

Joel Dahmen roared into Memphis brimming with confidence and ready to go. Golf had become fun again and he hoped to build on the momentum gained at the Nelson and Scottsdale Open.

Girlfriend Lona Skutt was happy because the bills were paid and she and Joel had splurged and made our "first major purchase". A vacuum cleaner. Everything was good.

***

The FedEx St. Jude Classic was started in 1958 and was first known as the Memphis Open. In 1970 it became the Danny Thomas Memphis Classic and St. Jude's Children's Hospital became the recipient charity. In 1986 Federal Express signed on as corporate sponsor and the tournament is generally regarded as the most successful charity event on tour. It was played at the Colonial Country Club until 1971 and is now held at TPC Southwind, a challenging par 70 course

As always, Joel Dahmen was paired with players in the "non-established" category for the first two rounds. Ryan Armour is a 40 year-old who has bounced around between the PGA and mini tours for many years and he is just a couple of notches below Joel in the FedEx standings. Xander Schauffele is 23 and slightly ahead of Joel in the ratings.

Golf-wise the first round was pretty routine for Dahmen. He made two birdies and two bogeys and shot an even par 70 which left him in a tie for 41st. He didn't have any three putts but couldn't seem to figure out the Bermuda greens and failed to convert several birdie opportunities inside 15 feet. But, he hit the ball well and was swinging with total confidence. He went to bed feeling a strong second round was a good possibility.

More importantly, there was something else in the air and both Joel and Geno felt it. "Today we weren't out there just trying to make a cut. Today we were out there trying to make birdies and move up the leaderboard. It's different and feels good," Bonnalie explained.

Matt Every, Scott Brown, Stewart Cink and Sebastin Munoz, whose caddie Danny Renneisen is one of Geno Bonnalie's frequent roommates, shared the first round lead with six under par 64's. Schauffele shot 69 and Armour posted a 73.

***

A confident Dahmen was bogey and three-putt free in the second round. The result was a solid 66 that left him in a tie for 18th and comfortably below the cut line of one over par. Playing companions Xander Schauffele and Bryan Armour shot 69 and 67, respectively, and both made the cut. Joel's fellow rookie and friend Sebastin Munoz continued his strong play and remained a co-leader at nine under par with former masters champion Charles Schwartzel and Chez Reavie, a 2005 winner of the RBC Canadian Open.

Dahmen and Bonnalie were excited. Joel's game was sharp and they were looking forward to the third round and their pairing with Bobby Gates and Brett Drewitt. Gates is 237th in FedEx Cup standing while Australian native Drewitt held the 189th position.

Essentially it was a scrambling, grind it out third round for Joel as his ball striking wasn't as good as the first two days. Still, he managed to salvage a very respectable 69 while Drewitt fired a 72 and Gates stumbled to a 77.

At day's end the veteran Cink was atop the leaderboard tied with Ben Crane and newcomer Rafael Cabrera Bello. Munoz had dropped out of contention with a 75 but Phil Mickelson had climbed back into the mix and like Joel, was four shots behind the co-leaders going into the final round.

***

TPC Southwind was showing is teeth and the 10 water hazards had all claimed a victim or two during the championship. On Saturday, Munoz and Charles Schwartzel were tied for the lead at one point and both hit tee shots in the water and made triple bogeys. On Sunday, Mickelson came out roaring and got within one shot of the lead before making his own triple on number 12.

Dahmen's playing companion for round four was Tyrone Van Aswegean, a 35 year-old South African who attained his US citizenship in 2013. He was sitting in the 119th position in the FedEx Cup rankings.

Joel had avoided the dreaded water all week but finally hit a crooked tee ball on 14 and then followed with two incredible recovery shots to salvage a bogey. Other than that, the round was solid if unspectacular and he finished with a 70 and Van Aswegan recorded a 73.

His final score was five under par and it left him in a tie for 18th place. This was worth $86,613 and the bank account was continuing to grow. It was also worth 44 valuable FedEx points.

***

WINNER'S CIRCLE - The current crop of young PGA Tigers is making the game more interesting and the likes of Rickie Fowler, Jason Day, Jordan Spieth and Rory McIlroy have become household names. Daniel Berger has begun to make the case that he also belongs on this list of young elite players.

Berger came from behind by shooting 66 – 66 on the weekend to win the championship for the second straight year. Berger, 24 years old, upped his FedEx ranking to 24th and his even, steady demeanor was drawing high praise from many golf insiders.

PART THREE

CHAPTER ONE
THE REGULAR SEASON'S FINAL STEPS

June 20, 2017

Joel Dahmen and Geno Bonnalie were still walking with Tigers but things seemed very different entering the stretch run of their rookie season on the PGA Tour.

In January, close friend Nick Taylor said "one weekend can change Joel's life forever," and it appeared that magical Sunday in Dallas when Joel had beaten Dustin Johnson had done just that. It was the first day Joel had ever been paired with a top fifty player and, despite nerves and the pressure of playing before a huge gallery, he had succeeded and earned his first top ten check on the PGA Tour. The $195,000 prize had cured a lot of ills.

Now the financial pressure was off of player and caddie alike. Joel was debt free with travel money for the rest of the season in the bank. Geno now had some money too. "I'm still cheap and will always look for bargain basement motels but I am going to splurge and keep it down to one or two roommates per trip. This should also help me get home with the right clothes," Geno laughed.

The next positive factor may be as important as the short-term financial security. For the rest of the year, the playing schedule is just that – a schedule. There will be no more long layoffs, Monday qualifying or uncertainty about getting into a particular event. Dahmen will not be eligible for the Quicken Loans National, the British Open or PGA Championship of course, but he is assured to be playing nine weeks in a row. Eight of those will be PGA events.

"It will be so nice to be able to count on playing week after week. Before now it seemed like every event was a brand new beginning and I couldn't get any rhythm or confidence going. I'm excited about a strong finish," Dahmen shared.

Bonnalie said essentially the same thing. "Joel and I both feel things are different. We never even thought about making/missing the cut in Memphis. Now, it's just climb the leaderboard. I know there are likely to be disappointing weeks in our future, but for now, I love where we are at. Hopefully we can ride this train for another 8 - 9 weeks and keep this PGA Tour card. The idea of going back to the Web.com Tour doesn't sound appealing after the last two weeks," Bonnalie explained.

There was a definite down side to this, however. Playing that many weeks in a row was going to be tiring and it was going to be tough for Joel to keep his mental focus intact. Nine weeks in a row of tournament golf was going to be an extremely tough challenge.

What will it take to keep the card? The sure bet and the method closest at hand is to finish in the top 125 in FedEx Cup points. Entering this stretch run, Joel was in the 162nd position with 126 points. Currently, the player ranked number 125 has 231 points.

With the mission clear, the final stage of the Tiger walk was about to begin.

CHAPTER TWO

JUNE 22 – 25
CROMWELL, CONNECTICUT

The Travelers Championship in the greater Hartford area is the second most attended tournament on the PGA Tour. Only the February stop in Phoenix attracts more spectators.

The event was founded by the Hartford Jaycees in 1952 and was initially played at the Weatherford Country Club. It was moved to the TPC River Highlands in 1991 and plays to a par 70 at 6841 yards. The tournament has had seven name changes since its inception, but early on was best known as the Sammy Davis, Jr. Greater Hartford Open. Travelers became corporate sponsor in 2007.

The tournament organizers go out of their way to make the players and caddies feel comfortable and they strive to be the best in the business when it comes to hospitality. Joel and Lona said they were succeeding. They have a special lobster bake dinner for players and their families on Thursday night and they are one of the few venues that has a special hospitality tent for family members. Plus, the volunteers make sure family members get inside the gallery ropes and attend to special requests quickly and efficiently. "It just runs very smoothly." Lona said.

The championship history of the event is perhaps best explained by looking at the golf royalty who have won the tournament multiple times. Included are Tigers such as Sam Snead, Arnold Palmer, Billy Casper, Lee Trevino, Paul Azinger, Greg Norman, Phil Mickelson and Bubba Watson. A jaw-dropping list for sure.

Russell Knox is the defending champion but the 2016 tournament is most remembered because Jim Furyk made golf history by shooting a 58 in the third round.

Contributing to the popularity of the Travelers is the excitement of the closing holes. Holes 15 - 17 are played around a four-acre lake and commentators have dubbed it the most thrilling finish on tour.

***

Joel Dahmen was invited to play in Monday's Pro Am and then joined buddies Mackenzie Hughes, Adam Hadwin and Nick Taylor for a comfortable practice round on Tuesday. This was a nice change for Joel as it gave him and caddie Geno Bonnalie two good looks at the course instead of the normal one.

Dahmen's pocket book and FedEx standings had improved in recent weeks but the rookie tee time scenario had stayed the same. In round one he would be last off the 10th tee at 2:00 pm playing with Chase Seiffert and Bobby Gates. Seiffert was a Monday qualifier and a Florida State roommate of Brooks Koepka, who had one the US Open the week before. Gates and Dahmen had been paired in third round of the St. Jude Tournament a couple of weeks ago and he was currently 237th in FedEx Cup points.

***

"Some days you feel golfey and some days you don't," - Marilyn Ruch retired Palm Springs golfer and life philosopher.

Joel never got confident or comfortable in the first two rounds of the event and struggled throughout. At one point in the second round, he was three under for the tournament but gave all of that back by making bogeys on three of the last five holes. The result was a 69 - 71 and he barely squeezed under the cut line of even par.

"Joel just wasn't sharp and, in the second round he was in a negative mindset. Basically, no phase of his game was very good and we had trouble chipping to the crowned greens that are a characteristic of the course. We are kind of lucky to be playing the weekend," said Geno Bonnalie.

Playing companion Gates struggled and his 80 - 72 was well over the cut line. Seiffert however shot 68 - 66 and his six under par put him in great position three strokes behind tournament leader Jordan Spieth.

***

Adam Hadwin often plays practice rounds with Joel and Nick Taylor leading up to tournaments and the three had played together on Tuesday. Hadwin, who is exempt because he won a tournament in 2015, is having a dream season. He won the Valspar in Florida and racked up a second place finish at the Career Builders Challenge in Palm Springs. To date he has won $2,800,000 and is a rock solid 11th in the FedEx Cup standings.

Hadwin is originally from Moose Jaw, Saskatchewan which makes him the butt of good natured teasing from his friends but there is nothing funny about his golf game which is solid in every respect. He has earned the right to be classified with the new breed of golfing Tigers.

Hadwin's success is another reason Joel and Geno have so much hope for the future. Joel often beats him (and Taylor too) in practice sessions so he stands as a perfect example of what Joel can become if he is able to start playing up to his ability.

The third round pairings put Joel and Hadwin with Grayson Murray, who has made 11 of 20 cuts this season and is currently 122nd in FedEx standings. Hadwin and Grayson shot 68 and 67, respectively and crawled up the leaderboard. Joel on the other hand went backwards with an uninspiring 71 which left him in a tie for last with Robert Streb. Those two would be first off the number one tee the next morning.

Interestingly, Joel three-putted his 17th hole. A simple two putt would have set him up to play with Rory McIlory in the final round.

***

WINNER'S CIRCLE - The final round of the Travelers gave further credence to three accepted facts. First, Jordan Spieth is flat out great. He had the tournament lead in all three of the early rounds and ended up winning the tournament by beating upcoming superstar Daniel Berger in a one-hole playoff. Berger had won in Memphis just two weeks prior.

This was Spieth's tenth PGA victory which places him between Tiger Woods and Jack Nicklaus for most career victories for a person under 24 years-old. Being mentioned in the same breath as Woods and Nicklaus is the ultimate compliment of greatness in the golf world. No higher praise is possible.

Second, in golf even the best often struggle under pressure. Spieth was fortunate to be in a playoff. He hit crooked tee shots and missed short putts and had to grind out an even par 70 to get the playoff spot. This brings up the third point – luck DOES play a part in golf.

Twice during his closing round Spieth hit shots that appeared to be water bound but were saved by high rough and plain old good luck. This was truly the case on 15 when he narrowly escaped the lake and then holed a 15 foot putt he thought he had mishit. But, the real capper was the playoff hole.

Spieth pull hooked his drive into a giant tree and the ball could have ended up just about anywhere including out-of-bounds. Instead, it hit the tree solid and bounced straight right and back in the fairway. Jordan didn't take advantage and hit his second shot right into a steep mound in the deep rough. This could have left him with an extremely hard pitch but the ball took a great bounce and ended up in a greenside bunker in a perfect lie. This time he did take advantage and holed the sand shot for the winning birdie!

***

Joel Dahmen and Robert Streb played their round in less than three hours and both moved up the leaderboard with scores of 69 and 68, respectively. This left Joel in a tie for 62nd worth \$14,484 and four FedEx points which dropped him one place in the yearly standings. Streb ended up tied for 57th with Hadwin. Chase Seiffert tied for 43rd and Grayson Murray moved all the way to 26th with a closing round 68. Nick Taylor missed the 36-hole cut finishing at six over and Sebastin Munoz missed the secondary cut and didn't get to play on Sunday.

CHAPTER THREE

JUNE 25
MANHATTAN

Joel, Geno and Lona had the rest of the day off and decided to make the short drive to Manhattan to have a little fun and take in the sites.

They attended *the Book of Mormon* play at a small off Broadway theatre and enjoyed a dinner and a couple of beverages at a small local place. There they met some golfers and Joel bought them a couple of pitchers of beer and the group had a pleasant conversation. They asked Joel what he did and he told them he was an accountant. "It's hilarious to me that he doesn't like people to know he plays on the PGA Tour. It's a great quality because he doesn't want to be the center of attention. I always like to brag on him, but I think he would have punched me if I told the truth," Geno laughed.

Bonnalie also joked about the sites around Broadway. "It's weird being the sheltered kid from Idaho and seeing gay parades, girls with beards, guys with boobs, etc. This kind of stuff doesn't bother me at all but I'm inclined to stare a little bit. We don't see much of that in Lewiston," he said.

The side trip was a good thing for the three friends. Joel had made some money at the Travelers but he didn't put together the kind of golf it took to enhance his position in FedEx standings. Disappointment was shared by player and caddie alike and some plain old fun kept them from dwelling on the missed opportunity.

CHAPTER FOUR

JUNE 29 – JULY 2
NASHVILLE, TENNESSEE

The fifth and second to last PGA approved invitational tournament was being held in the Washington, DC area this week. Named the Quicken Loans for its corporate sponsor, the tournament is in its tenth year. Tiger Woods has always been the tournament host but this year he is in rehabilitation for drug addiction which came to light after last month's DUI charge.

The tournament is special because it raises major money for the Tiger Woods Foundation which sponsors several on the nation's most effective programs for low income youth. Also, Tiger started the tournament as a way to honor the men and women of the armed forces and many caddie, starter and announcer duties are handled by military people. Further, the feeling of patriotism is greatly enhanced because any person in uniform gets free admittance to all tournament functions.

The invitational tournaments are perfect examples of how the golfing establishment makes things tough on rookies. The invitational fields are always limited, this time 120 players got in. So, non-established players like Joel either take the week off or play in a Web.com event.

***

Joel Dahmen and Geno Bonnalie decided to make lemonade out of lemons by entering the Web.com tournament and making it a working vacation with Holly Bonnalie flying in to be part of the fun. This was especially welcome because this was Holly's first chance to get out of Lewiston for a 2017 road trip. Luckily, the venue was perfect because Nashville is a favorite of the

Bonnalie's, Dahmen and Lona Skutt. The four friends were ready for live music, good food and drink, a lot of laughs and a little golf.

Contributing to the great mindset was the fact that the four of them were the guests of Scotty and Julie Haynes who own a beautiful and comfortable place in the area. Scotty has done some business investing with Bob Yosaitis, Joel's sponsor and close friend. He and a friend were also Pro-Am playing partners who gave Geno pro shop gift certificates worth $1000. "I've now got golf shorts for the next two years," Geno said thankfully.

***

Joel and Geno had an early tee time on Thursday morning and were surprised to see two familiar and friendly faces waiting for them on the first tee.

Last year, Holly and Lona were following play in the opening round when they saw a young boy in the gallery pass out. Holly went over and said to the father, "I'm not a practicing nurse but I am a trained one and I'll help." She immediately saw that the boy was suffering from heat exhaustion and called Joel and Geno over to get water and snacks from the golf bag. Joel and Geno also offered encouragement and Holly stayed with the pair until an ambulance arrived to take him to the hospital.

They were forever grateful and said "we have been Joel Dahmen fans ever since. We follow him on the internet all the time and are thrilled to be here again to see you guys live," the father smiled. They followed Joel during the first two rounds.

***

Joel's opening round included eight birdies and two bogeys resulting in solid six under par. This left him tied for second behind Conrad Shindler, a Texas A & M grad currently rated ninth on the Web.com money list, who shot a course record 62 at the Nashville Golf and Athletic Club. Joel's playing companions were two guys far down the Web.com money list. Englishman Ben Taylor shot a two over par 74 and Argentinian Puma Dominguez had 76.

"On Thursday I really felt we were going to steam roll everyone in the field and I was almost right. We felt sharp and at six under, we were in great shape," said Bonnalie.

Everyone was feeling good about the day and Thursday night the four friends joined Bo and Jen Hargett for a nice dinner and some live music on Broadway. The Hargett's had hosted Joel and Geno in Evansville, Indiana last year during a Web Tour event.

***

The good feel and outlook Dahmen had in round one disappeared on Friday. On a day where a couple of under par would have been good, Dahmen went the other way with an ugly three-over 75 which put him three under for the tournament and only one stroke better than the cut line. Also, he was now eight shots behind leader Shindler who managed a one under par 71. Meanwhile, Joel's playing partners both missed the cut. Taylor ended up 74 – 77 while Dominguez had a 76 – 70.

***

This Web.com tournament is officially called the National Golf Open Benefitting the Snedeker Foundation. This charity was established by PGA stalwart and established Tiger Brendt Snedeker and his wife Mandy to benefit the kids of middle Tennessee. The Snedekers are also active in playing the role of tournament hosts and are highly visible during the week.

A big topic of conversation during the week was that NBA superstar Stephen Curry announced he would be playing under a special sponsor exemption in the upcoming Ellie Mae Web tournament to be played in the San Francisco Bay area next month. Many Web players were looking forward to the extra attention Curry would bring to their tournament especially in the Bay area where the Curry followers are numerous and enthusiastic. Others were unhappy because he would be keeping a more deserving player out of the field. Regardless of one's opinion, there was no mistake that Curry's news created a buzz in the locker room and on the driving range.

***

Saturday's third round with Frank Adams III, who had made his first cut on the Web.com Tour, and Tain Lee, ranked 35th in Web tour winnings, went a little better than Friday. Joel was back to hitting the ball solid but the putts wouldn't fall and the two under par 70 moved him to five under par but still seven behind Shindler who was clinging to a one-shot lead. Adams moved to five under with a 70 and Tain's 71 put him at minus four heading to the final round.

***

The humidity in Nashville had been relentless all week and a tired field of golfers and caddies made their way to club for Sunday's final round. Joel was again paired with Adams and Dan Woltman currently ranked 134th on the Web.com money list.

On the way to the course Joel and Geno decided to stop at Waffle House for breakfast. The chain restaurant is huge in the southeast part of the United States and was a made famous to many in the rest of the country because of its role in the popular golf movie *Tin Cup*. The server was wearing a silly looking paper hat and Geno ask him if he had a spare one. The server gave him several and Geno decided to wear one to bring extra mojo to the day. Joel joined in and donned one too and they were a smash hit. "Everyone was taking pictures and people were yelling things at us. We were just being silly but it turned out to be a cool deal. Who knows, maybe Waffle house will throw us some free food," Dahmen said.

Maybe the hats were cool but the triple bogey on the second hole wasn't. It made any kind of a huge upward move impossible and the round was more work than fun. The siren for lightning blew when Dahmen had three holes left. At this point, a long delay awaited them, Geno was going to get soaked because caddies were not allowed in the locker room, and they were at the bottom of the leaderboard. These factors made finishing seem pointless because they were going to get the minimum make the cut check anyway and they had a long drive ahead to get to the next event. So, they picked up and enjoyed a pleasant evening with their hosts.

Playing companions Woltman and Adams did finish shooting 69 and 72, respectively. Woltman ended tied for 38th and Adams tied for 50th.

Meanwhile, the finish of the tournament turned out to be a very big deal for a couple of players. Abraham Ancer fired a five under par 67 in the second round and tied Lanto Griffin who finished with a 68. This left them tied at 16 under par and Griffin claimed the title with a birdie on the first playoff hole. During his opponent's rallies, Shindler, who led after each of the first three rounds faltered and his 75 dropped him into a tie for 24th.

This was Lanto Griffin's first Web.com win and it moved him to second place on the money list. It was also Ancer's best finish ever and he jumped to number 11 in the important tour rating.

***

The Nashville week was a huge success if measured by fun. Good friends enjoying each other, great food and drink, wonderful hosts and first-class country music can make for a wonderful week.

But the mission ahead was golf, not fun. In that regard it is tough to put lipstick on the pig. Bottom line is Joel barely made the cut and finished tied for last in a Web.com tournament. Though talented, this field was weak when compared to PGA events where the real Tigers lurk. Unless he picked it up substantially, Joel Dahmen would not be playing on the PGA Tour next year.

CHAPTER FIVE

JULY 6 – 9
WHITE SULPHAR SPRINGS, WEST VIRGINIA

The Old White TPC course is part of the world class Greenbrier Resort in the Alleghany Mountains in southeast West Virginia. It is an eight hour drive from Nashville. The course, like the resort is first-class all the way and was the sight of the 1979 Ryder Cup matches. However, there was some concern about the course this year because it was totally washed out in a huge flood last year. In fact, the flood had caused cancellation of the 2016 tournament.

In 2010, the Greenbrier had replaced the old Buick Open as a regular tour stop and it had become a favorite of the players and their families due to the beauty and wealth of activities available in the area. Also, the players have the privilege of staying in the main resort hotel, an option not afforded their caddies.

Supposedly, the owner of the resort buys up all the hotel rooms in the small town and jacks all the prices through the roof. This makes it impossible to find a decent rate which is a real problem for "thrifty" guys like Geno Bonnalie and his friend and frequent roommate Danny Renneisen. Luckily, Danny had asked the tour travel planners for some help and they secured a very nice host family.

Gloria and Bill Yates were gracious people happy to help out and they welcomed Danny and Geno to their home for the week. The house was a small one and Geno had a bed suitable for a dwarf but the price was right. The four of them would be sharing one shower in a room where the door didn't close all the way. Also they were warned "don't turn the fan and light on at the same time because it will short out the breaker."

Joel and Lona were living quite differently this week. Their facility was four-star all the way. Luckily, Geno is not a jealous person and Joel didn't rub it in. At least not too much.

The isolation of the Greenbrier and the fact that almost all of the players were staying at the same hotel created some special rare opportunities for the people to socialize as a unit. The bar and casino were full of players and their families each night and Joel and Lona enjoyed the atmosphere and fellowship very much. Also, the hotel put on a gala fireworks show leading Joel to comment "there is no place better to celebrate being an American than the Greenbrier on the fourth of July."

Earlier in the day, Joel and veteran Ken Duke met Nick Taylor and MacKenzie Hughes for a practice round and they challenged the two Canadians to a bet on their country's birthday. On this July 4th the Canadians easily prevailed and lightened the pockets of their American friends.

***

One can't visit the Greenbrier and not be fascinated by its history especially the true story of the secret bunker. In the 1950's Americans were fearful that a nuclear war would become a possibility and some older US citizens remember frequent bomb drills at school. Students were taught to get under their desks, cover their heads and stay put until an all clear alarm was sounded.

President Eisenhower worried about how to keep law and order in America in the aftermath of a nuclear war and he decided a bunker was needed to house the members of the Senate and House of Representatives and he picked Greenbrier as the perfect location. In 1958 ground was broken on the project known as Project Greek Island. Hotel workers were told the giant hole in the ground would house a new conference facility. In fact, part of the hole was used for that but the rest became a huge dormitory, food storage area and secret safe place.

Part of the amazement of this project was that it was kept secret until 1992 when it was finally exposed. Before that, bankers, industrialists, political figures and the rich and famous hobnobbed at the resort, not knowing that right next door was the post-apocalyptic bunker.

WALKING WITH TIGERS

***

Joel Dahmen's golf game looked like it was back on track four weeks ago but, in the beautiful mountains of West Virginia, he laid an egg for the third straight tournament. In Thursday's opening round he didn't make a single birdie en route to a 71 and Friday's second round was mediocre at best and he ended with an even par 70. This left him a shot below the cut line so there would be no money or FedEx points.

Once again, the culprit was Joel's short game. He lost over three strokes to the field in putting statistics and that tells the story.

Still, Dahmen found a silver lining. During a stretch on Friday, he made three birdies in a row and felt he was "pretty close" to playing well.

Meanwhile, others were having an easy time with Greenbrier. Joel's playing companions were Jonathan Randolph and Seamus Power, two players who, like Dahmen, were trying to break into the top 125 in the FedEx Cup standings. Randolph who is sitting in the 150th spot had 67 – 68 and Power who is 142nd, recorded a 68 – 71. Friend Nick Taylor was also in great shape and sat seven under par after the two rounds.

But, the real news so far was Renneisen's player, fellow rookie Sebastin Munoz who was flat out lighting it up! Munoz had a sizzling 61 on Thursday and his 67 on Friday put him at 12 under par, three shots ahead of Hudson Swafford and Ben Martin.

***

Sebastin Munoz might be 410 in the world rankings but his thirty-six hole lead was not a surprise to some including his caddie Danny Renneisen, Geno Bonnalie's friend and current roommate. Munoz had led the St. Jude event in Memphis at the halfway mark before fading away in round three. But, on this day there was no fade. He shot a solid 68 and retained his lead after three rounds.

Renneisen and Geno decided to celebrate with a couple of cold beers and a sandwich at a nearby Irish Pub. It was impossible not to be excited about the next day.

Two shots behind was Robert Streb who, like Munoz, was dreaming of a big, career-making day. Streb was currently ranked 137th in FedEx Cup standings so a solid finish would put him well inside the coveted 125.

Sunday's round was going to be a pressure-filled final day for the two rookies. Especially since two other young, hungry Tigers were only three shots behind and ready to pounce. Those were James Lovemark and Xander Schauffele ranked 63rd and 94th in the FedEx standings.

Meanwhile, Taylor was sitting in 7th place at 8 under par, Randolph shot 70 in the third round and was tied for 16th and Power had rallied with a 67 and moved up to 26th.

***

The Greenbrier has a special distinction that adds to final day drama for young players. The top four finishers, who were not qualified by other criteria, receive an entry to the British Open. An invitation to one of golf's four majors is a dream come true to most young players and amps up the pressure a notch.

Munoz' putting stroke was magical in the first three rounds but it deserted him early in the final round and he missed four short putts on the front nine. But, he recovered beautifully with birdies on holes 11 and 12 and was right back in the thick of things with seven holes to go.

The other three young guns were also playing well and the championship was up for grabs down the stretch. All four golfers were tied for the lead or only a shot behind with three holes to go.

Nick Faldo, one of the CBS announcers, said the par five 17th hole would likely determine the winner. But, it didn't work out that way. Munoz, Streb, Schauffele and Lovemark all hit great drives and all had either hybrids or long irons to the green. Curiously, all four hit weak second shots and there were no birdies at all on the course's easiest hole.

The 18th is a par three and Schauffele, playing in the second to the last group, knocked his tee shot three feet from the hole and made the tournament winning birdie putt. He was the eight first time winner on tour this year.

Though disappointed, the other three competitors were very well

WALKING WITH TIGERS

rewarded for their great play. All made a nice bundle of cash, jumped up the FedEx standings and were headed to the British Open! They had accomplished what Joel Dahmen didn't. The Greenbrier had put them in great position to keep their PGA cards. The following shows the importance of their strong performance:

Player	Previous FedEx Rank	New Position
Schauffele	94	27
Streb	137	68
Lovemark	63	41
Munoz	198	162

CHAPTER SIX

JULY 9 – 16
SILVIS, ILLINOIS

Getting from the Greenbrier to Silvis, Illinois can be quite challenging. Player Joel Dahmen and caddie Geno Bonnalie arrived in very different manners.

Joel and Lona jumped on a special charter flight and, along with about 70 others Greenbrier participants, flew into a private airport on Sunday afternoon. By Sunday night they had eaten a nice dinner and were snuggly bedded down in a Holiday Inn Express.

Geno and buddy Danny Reinnesen left by car on Sunday night and settled in for a 15 – 17 hour drive. They made it to Dayton, Ohio about midnight on Sunday, grabbed a few hours of sleep and then went the rest of the way on Monday. They checked into a La Quinta Hotel along with TJ Rice, Brett Dewitt's caddie. It was like old times. Three guys, two beds, one shower, low rates. Right in Geno's wheelhouse.

But, Geno and Danny actually enjoyed the drive. The two friends had much to discuss and "we cranked up the music and let 'er rip," said Bonnalie. Plus, Danny was still on a high from being in the final group at the Greenbrier and coming very close to winning the golf tournament. His player Sebastin Munoz had tied for third and pocketed a cool $400,000 and earned a trip to the British Open. Danny had been hoping for a win but third was a huge deal for the rookie player and his caddie.

Meanwhile, Sebastin's immediate future was up in the air. The Colombian citizen would be spending Tuesday in Chicago trying to get a passport so that he could go to Europe. He was hoping this moved quickly because he wanted to play in this John Deere tournament prior to leaving for the UK. At this moment he was at the mercy of the visa police.

Joel's swing instructor Rob Rashell had flown in and met him at the range the following morning. They reviewed some fundamentals and then made some changes to Joel's putting approach. First, they flattened his putter because Rashell was sure the current loft was getting the putts to wobble off line from the very first contact. Next, they changed his grip slightly, moved the ball back in his stance and added a pronounced forward press. These seemed to feel good and Joel was pleased with the way he was rolling the ball.

Rashell would also be with Dahmen for his practice round on Tuesday with Canadian buddies MacKenzie Hughes and Nick Taylor and Wednesday for another practice session.

"He looks good but he is tired. The schedule has been grueling and certainly none of the top guys would recommend playing this much golf without a break. I know he has no choice given his status but it makes top finishes that much harder because of the mental fatigue. I think this more than the quality of his golf game is the major reason for the recent downturn. His mechanics are as strong as ever," Rashell added.

Rashell went on "Joel is going to be fine. His swing is good and tinkering with it would be going down a slippery slope. He doesn't need to beat balls all day because that approach has not gotten him to where he is. Sometimes I watch him hit 15 or 20 balls and say okay let's go chip and putt."

***

The John Deere Classic has been held at the TPC Deere Run in Silvis, Illinois since 2000. The tourney was founded in 1971 as the Quad Cities Open until Deere stepped in as corporate sponsor in 1999.

The quad cities area is about 165 miles west of Chicago and consists of four counties in northwest Illinois and southeast Iowa. The metropolitan area has a population just short of 400,000 and consists of Davenport and Bettendorf, Iowa and Rock Island and Moline, Illinois. The golf course in Silvis is a suburb and is within a few miles of the John Deere corporate offices.

The Classic has an unenviable spot on the PGA Tour schedule. It is held a week before the British Open and every year it loses countless top players who head to the UK early to prepare for the season's third major. Tournament officials have done everything they can to entice players to stay and play going so far as to charter a jet to the UK for those who play here and have qualified for the Open. So, in was a real blow when two-time champion Jordan Spieth announced he would skip the tournament.

In the past, the Deere leadership has tried some gimmicks to promote interest and twice they invited teenager Michelle Wie to play on a special sponsor's exemption. She represented herself fairly well but didn't make the cut either time and her appearances caused some controversy. Her participation did spark interest and attendance was up when she played but others felt taking a spot away from a young more deserving male player was unfair.

The good news was three local favorites did enter the event and were expected to have collective drawing power. Zach Johnson is a Ryder Cup player and legitimate PGA star who also happens to be from the area. He is also a past champion. Steve Stricker, a future Hall-of-Fame player has won the event three times and is very popular here. Plus, crowd favorite Bubba Watson is one of the tour's most exciting players and is a big draw wherever he goes.

***

The PGA players voted the Deere Classic as the number one tournament on tour. This was their second year in a row to get this recognition and it seemed a bit odd that they would get this designation when so many players skipped the event. Joel and Lona gave their views.

The Deere Company always invites players and their families to a Tuesday night barbeque at their corporate offices. Prior to the food service, the guest are invited to drive and tryout all of the equipment including many pieces that are heavy equipment used in major construction projects. Dahmen said "this was great fun and I've got a picture of Lona moving dirt with an earthmover."

The volunteers also drew praise from Dahmen who said "people go out of their way to make you comfortable and they work at remembering your name and being extremely friendly. They also put on a little Pro Am tournament on Saturday for those who miss the cut and we have a great time playing with nice people and competing for a little side money," he added.

***

Dahmen's playing companions for the first two rounds were one familiar face and one new one. Brad Fritsch, a 39-year-old Canadian, got his PGA card the same way as Dahmen, they were in the top 25 on the Web.com Tour last season. They had met often and Fritsch was paired with Joel in his first PGA event in Mississippi. He is 197th on the FedEx list and his best finish this season is a tie for 29th. David Lawrence is a local professional playing on his home course under a sponsor's exemption.

Unfortunately, all three of these players missed the 36-hole cut of two under par on the par 71 course. Joel had 74 – 73, Fritsch went 72 – 71 and Lawrence tallied rounds of 73 – 68. Others struggled as well and both of Geno Bonnalie's roommates missed the cut as well. Munoz got his visa but shot 73 – 68 and Dewitt carded a 71 – 73. Even the consistent Nick Taylor stumbled with rounds of 76 – 69.

Featured player Stricker barely made the cuts with rounds of 73 – 67 and Watson was a stroke better with scores of 69 – 70. However, local favorite Johnson was in the thick of things with 65 – 67 which left him two strokes behind halfway leader Patrick Rodgers who sat at 13 under par.

***

Joel's game included some uncharacteristic pull hooks that resulted in penalty shots. During his practice sessions with Rashell, he worked on squaring up his body so that it would be more aligned to the actual target line. Dahmen had begun to aim a bit right (closed) and Rashell felt this was causing some inconsistency at impact. Joel felt comfortable right away during practice sessions but, under the heat of tournament pressure, he was not able to fully conform to the slight adjustment and this resulted in the wayward shots.

Still, Joel felt the time with Rashell would pay dividends. The new putting method had worked okay and he was getting more and more comfortable to the slight setup change. He put the Deere effort behind him and was anxious to get to the next stop.

***

The cut was missed but Joel and caddie Geno had nowhere to go because they were not booked on any flights until Monday. After Friday's second round, Geno, Renneisen and Ryan Blaums caddie, Todd Montoya, played at Crow Valley and were greeted with first-rate hospitality. They had a good time and decided to return Saturday afternoon. They were paired with a couple of members and enjoyed a few drinks after the round. This led to an under the lights putting contest until nearly midnight before Geno ended it by making a 100 footer to win $80.

One down side to recreational golf is that Geno, suffering from Plantar fasciitis, plays in constant foot pain even though he uses a golf cart whenever possible. The pain gets worse when he is on his feet for extended periods so his caddie sessions are often unpleasant. Still, Geno presses on without ever complaining because his love of golf and desire to help Joel trump all discomfort.

***

WINNER'S CIRCLE – Former US Amateur champion and PGA rookie Bryson DeChambeau came from four shots behind third round leader Patrick Rodgers to claim his first tournament victory. This was the 19th time the John Deere Classic had produced a first-time winner it and continued the trend of rookies dominating PGA events. DeChambeau became the 11th player to be a first time winner this season

The win gave DeChambeau the coveted two-year exemption plus a seat on the special charter headed for Royal Birkdale, site of next week's British Open.

DeChambeau said the victory was an affirmation for his somewhat unorthodox methods that have been criticized in some circles. He has been known as obsessive about things such as physics principles, attack angles and standard club lengths. Regardless, physics or no, he is now a winner on the PGA Tour and has the trophy and seat on the charter to prove it.

Three-time champion Steve Stricker had made Friday's 36 hole cut at two under par but rallied in the final two rounds to end up at 15 under par, three shots behind DeChambeau. Local hero Zach Johnson rallied early Saturday and was in contention before dropping back into a tie with Stricker. Bubba Watson was never a factor and finished six shots back.

CHAPTER SEVEN

JULY 17 – 23
AUBURN, ALABAMA

Getting from the Iowa – Illinois border to the southeast corner of Alabama is pretty challenging. But, Joel Dahmen, Geno Bonnalie and Lona Skutt got in a rental car and set off with Geno at the wheel. They covered the 165 miles to Chicago in easy fashion and dropped off Lona who decided to spend the week with a friend. Joel and Geno caught a non-stop flight to Birmingham and then jumped in another rental and made their way to Auburn, just a few miles west of the Georgia border.

In some ways the drive was like old times for Joel and Geno. It was just the two of them and it reminded them of their early days on the Web.com Tour when they often made long drives together to rural tournament sights. It also gave cause for Geno to repeat one of his old stories about his dear friend.

Geno was driving their rental car from the golf course to their motel in Columbus, Ohio. They got in the middle of a huge traffic snarl and weren't moving at all. Joel had to pee and he finally got to the point he could no longer hold it so he grabbed an empty coke bottle from the drink cups on the console and discretely relieved himself. He then recapped the bottle and returned it to the drink holder.

A couple of days passed and the two were once again inside the car on their way to the motel. Suddenly, Joel commented that he was really thirsty and asked if they had anything to drink. Before Geno could answer, Joel spied the coke bottle and took a large swallow before he remembered it was the same bottle he had used to relieve himself a couple of days before. Naturally, Geno howled with laughter and still does every time he remembers the look on Joel's face at the moment realization set in.

WALKING WITH TIGERS

***

Auburn, Alabama is smack in the middle of football country and the home town university's rivalry with the University of Alabama is considered to get the fiercest in all of college sports. Auburn University is also the area's dominant economic contributor and its 4300 employees are about 25% of the total work force in the area.

The Barbasol Champions tournament started in 2015 and it is considered a "minor tournament" because it is scheduled at the same time as the British Open and very few of the world's top players enter. The PGA awards only one-half of the normal FedEx points for this field and the prize fund is $3,500,000, compared to over $7,000,000 at the Travelers. Still, it represents a golden opportunity for the participants because the winner gets the standard two-year exemption that comes with all PGA tournament championships.

Jim Furyk was the best known player competing this week because, for the first time in 22 years, he was not eligible for the British Open.

The field may be weaker than normal but the golf course is not weak at all. The Grand National course is part of Alabama's Robert Trent Jones Trail and the accomplished Jones, Sr. said it is the greatest site for a golf complex he had ever seen.

***

The **Robert Trent Jones Golf Trail** is the largest golf course construction project ever attempted. In the late 1980's, two important things were on the mind of Dr. David Bronner, CEO of the Retirement Systems of Alabama. First, how to effectively diversify the assets of the state's pension fund; and secondly, how to help the state of Alabama. His philosophy was this: "The stronger the Retirement Systems can make Alabama, the stronger the Retirement Systems will be."

With that in mind, and borrowing a page from the movie, *Field of Dreams*, Bronner decided to "build it and they will come" — not to a baseball diamond in a cornfield, but to a dazzling collection of public golf courses in the state of Alabama.

Bronner's idea was to use a hot (but clean-burning) vehicle like golf to boost tourism, attract retirees, and spur economic growth within the state. His vision was on a grand scale — big, really big. "I don't do windows and I don't do just 18's." Dr. Bronner wasn't looking to build just an 18 hole public golf course, he wanted to build 378 holes at eight spectacular sites throughout the entire state, and all at one time!

When you're looking for someone to design 18 golf courses, start at the top. Enter legendary architect Robert Trent Jones, Sr., arguably the premier golf course architect in the world. In his unparalleled career Jones had designed more than 500 golf courses around the world, many of which are listed among *Golf Digest's* "America's 100 Greatest Golf Courses." Jones jumped at the chance and emerged from semi-retirement to tackle the project.

After all eight sites were opened, construction began on two new sites and was completed in 2005, expanding the Trail to 10 different sites. The historic Lakewood Golf Club in Point Clear has undergone extensive renovations and is the Trail's latest addition, bringing the total to 11 Trail sites...26 courses...and 468 incredible holes!

One of the most unique aspects of the Trail is the tee locations. The tee markers on the Trail are pegged to ability level, not age or gender. The courses were designed to measure as short as 4,700 yards and as long as about 8,200 yards from the tournament tees, with as many as 12 tee boxes in-between. The courses offer a tremendous amount of flexibility. As one Director of Golf put it, "The Robert Trent Jones Golf Trail is an incredible golfing experience for everyone. The courses will challenge the best golfers in the world, yet at the same time allow an enjoyable outing for the casual to beginning golfer."

Sunbelt Golf Corporation's philosophy from the very beginning was to build the finest collection of public golf courses in the world, and run them as a successful business investment. Indeed, the Robert Trent Jones Golf Trail is a dream come true for the people of Alabama and for golfers all over the world. There is no place quite like it.

WALKING WITH TIGERS

***

Joel and Geno were very impressed with the beauty of the golf course and they agreed the Trail might be an ideal place for a great golf vacation. But, the middle of summer is not the time to go there. The temperatures were in the 80's but the humidity was a killer. The tournament officials had coolers full of water and sport drinks sitting on almost every tee and it was a good thing. Geno was grabbing something on every hole and the two of them usually drained it before the hole was complete.

Joel played his usual practice round on Tuesday and then worked on his short game Wednesday. He was anxious to see if the work he had put in prior to the John Deere would pay off this week. He was hopeful he could take the setup changes from the practice tee and incorporate them on the golf course. Plus, the end of the season was fast approaching and he was running out of time to move up the FedEx point ladder.

So Joel was anxious to tee it up and get going. His playing partners for the first two rounds were 45 year-old veteran Steven Alker from New Zealand and 19 year old SM Lee, an amateur playing on a sponsor's exemption.

Unfortunately, Dahmen's recent slump continued in the weather delayed first round. In stifling humidity he got off to a poor start with a three over par 74 which left him near the bottom of the leaderboard and in an unlikely position to make the cut. His troubles continued on the front nine in round two and reached a low point when he made a silly double bogey on the par four seventh hole.

He decided to try a risky tee shot that required a slight hook around a group of trees. He hit the shot but it didn't hook as much as he wanted and both he and Geno thought the ball had ended up in the lake near the green. So, Joel hit another tee shot and then hit a wedge to the green. When they got closer to the cup, they saw Dahmen's original tee shot right next to the green in perfect position to make a birdie or, at worst a par. This was truly an unforced two or three stroke error and destroyed any reasonable chance of making the cut.

Then, perhaps feeling all the pressure was off, Joel got on a major roll on the back side. He hit an iron to four feet on 11 and made the putt for his first birdie. On 13, a wedge to nine feet resulted in another birdie and then he hit a spectacular second shot on the par five 16th and knocked in a nine foot putt for eagle. He capped the rally on the 207 yard par three 17th when he hit his iron to four feet and dropped the putt. The strong finish left him at one under through 36 holes but the cut was two under. So for the fourth tournament in a row he earned no money or FedEx points.

Amateur Lee also finished his 36 holes at one under but Bonnalie called him "a future star who would have easily made the cut if his caddie would have been any help at all. That kid is going to be on tour soon. He has incredible talent," Bonnalie added.

Alker caught fire early in round one and sat at nine under par in a tie for sixth place when the second day was completed. "He put on a clinic on iron play that was flat out was spectacular. If he would have putted well he would have been even higher in the standings," Bonnalie observed.

The halfway leader was Chad Collins who shot an eleven under 60 in the second round and had a four shot lead over the field heading to Saturday's round three.

***

WINNER'S CIRCLE – Grayson Murray became the latest rookie to win a PGA event and gain the two-year exemption that goes with victory. This seems almost common place this season as the rookies seem to be dominating a high percentage of the events. Murray became the fifth player from Joel Dahmen's exemption class to win a tournament this season and he is now set regardless of what he does in the upcoming months.

Murray started the final round one behind Scott Stallings but closed with a 68 and edged early leader Chad Collins by one shot. Stallings finished two behind. The hot starting Alker faded in the last two rounds and ended up in a tie for 42nd worth $11,326.

The 23-year-old Murray had become a polarizing figure as he has tweeted irreverent messages to a playboy model, his fellow professionals, the world's ranking system, the physical appearance of a high school student, a mid-round split with his caddie, internet trolls and police shootings. In a sport celebrated for its decorum, Murray has emerged as a polarizing antihero. He is either crude or complex, selfish or generous, ill-informed or misunderstood.

Despite this many people are amazed by what he has accomplished. Murray takes medicine for depression and anxiety disorders which is truly newsworthy because intense anxiety seems to go hand in hand with the pressures of professional golf.

How Murray handles his success will be as interesting as the man himself.

CHAPTER EIGHT
HARSH REALITY

"Winning isn't everything, it's the only thing"

This famous quote was attributed to the great Green Bay Packer football coach Vince Lombardi but it was likely stolen by Lombardi from UCLA football coach Red Sanders who used it a pregame speech in 1950. Regardless, harsh reality now made the saying appropriate for Joel Dahmen's immediate future on the PGA Tour.

Those players who finish in the top 125 in FedEx Cup points are assured of getting a fully exempt status for the next season and are assured of getting in the top tournaments.

Following the St. Jude tournament in early June, Dahmen appeared to be in a good position to secure one of those spots. He had climbed to 163rd in the standings after good finishes in Dallas and Memphis and his game seemed to be getting stronger. He definitely had momentum and, for the very first time all year, his schedule was favorable. He was in the field for seven of the nine next tournaments and most of those had weaker than normal fields because most of the world's biggest Tigers were taking time off to get ready for majors or more prestigious events. All of these factors seemed to be in Joel's favor and a potential strong move up the FedEx leaderboard seemed very possible.

Unfortunately, the hope for a strong and consistent surge fizzled with a poor performance at the Travelers and missed cuts at the Greenbrier, John Deere and Barbasol. Any realistic chance of crawling into the top 125 was gone because three regular season tournaments were left and one of them had reduced FedEx points.

This meant Joel's only path to an unrestricted exemption for next season was an outright victory in one of the remaining tournaments. This was a tall order but not impossible. This season five members of his exemption classification had secured a win and the exemption perks that go with it.

Joel's status outside the top 125 put him in good company and the list of top players also outside the mark was one indicator of how difficult competing with Tigers can be. Ben Crane, Bo Weekley, Angel Cabrera, Justin Leonard, YE Yang, Jerry Kelly, Stuart Appleby, KJ Choi, Hunter Mahan, Vijay Singh and Padraig Harrington were a few top players on the outside looking in. Some of them had other exemption statuses but others were on the bubble and in danger of losing their card.

However, some of Joel's classification mates, category 26 Top Finishers on the Web.com Tour, were faring quite well and about 20% of them were safely below the 125th player cut line. They included Kelly Kraft, CT Pan, Ollie Schniederjans, JJ Spaun, Ryan Blaum, Whee Kim, Bryson DeChambeau, Trey Mullinax, Xander Schauffele and Kevin Tway.

***

There is another way for a player to keep his PGA card but it is cumbersome and the classification status gained is restricted. This means the player can earn PGA privileges but will not be able to get in the fields of some of the high paying, high prestige tournaments. This results in limited opportunities and some long periods with no competition, income or FedEx opportunities. These are the same problems Joel faced this year so essentially it means his status will be much like the current season.

This alternate method is successful participation in the Web.com playoffs. Those eligible are PGA players ranked 126 – 200 in the FedEx standings (Joel is ranked 174th) plus those who finished from 26 – 75 on the Web.com money list. These players compete in a four-week tournament and the top 25 get the limited participation status for next PGA season. Those who finish above the top 25 can go back to the Web.com.

Obviously, winning one of these spots is not ideal but it beats the alternative of spending another full season trying to fight one's way back to the PGA. For some, that could become a career killer. At best, it would be a major setback.

The differences between playing on the PGA vs. the Web.com Tour are dramatic. It cost about $120,000 for a player to cover expenses on the PGA and about $75,000 on the Web. So, the expenses aren't a whole lot different but the potential payoffs certainly are. Some examples:

- The leading money winner on the Web is Andrew Landry with $276,118 in earnings this season. Jordan Spieth leads the PGA with over $6,700,000.
- 174 PGA players have earned more money than Landry including Joel who has garnered $319,000 and has one top 20 finish.
- 35 Web players have earned over the $75,000 so, in theory, all the rest aren't even covering expenses. The PGA has 210 players who have earned over $120,000.
- The normal prize pool for Web events is $600,000. The normal PGA pot is ten times that.
- Most Web events are not televised so endorsement deals are one-third as big, if not smaller than those available to the PGA guys.
- PGA events are played on some of the best, most manicured courses in the world. This isn't always true on the Web.
- PGA players are fed either breakfast, lunch or both every day. Sometimes caddies get food as well. This is a rather rare perk on the Web.

Additionally, it is not financially feasible for someone like Geno Bonnalie to serve as a full-time caddie on the Web. Salaries are negotiated between player and caddie but in general, Web caddies are paid significantly less than PGA caddies because the prize money available doesn't justify a higher salary. This is the case with Joel and Geno.

Because of this, and the fact that caddies have to cover their travel costs, trips to venues in South America, Mexico, etc. are not economically feasible for the caddie. This was faced by Joel and Geno during their year together on the Web which meant that Joel had to use other people to carry his bag and none were as capable or as moxie as Geno.

Bottom line is neither man wanted to go back to the Web.com which certainly intensified the pressure at hand.

***

The slump had been discouraging for sure and Joel was not happy about it. But, nobody ever said this would be easy. Swing coach Rob Rashell made some very strong points in assessing the year to date. "I tell Joel to think about the positives. He has more than covered expenses, survived the travels and new venues, made cuts, contended on the last day of a tournament, played with the top player in the world and was the first round co-leader of a PGA tournament on one of the toughest golf courses in the country. He can compete out here!" Rashell reminded.

"Plus, few players come right out in their rookie season and become stars. For every Tiger Woods, Phil Mickelson or Jordan Spieth, there are ten or twenty other guys that have taken years to make it," Rashell added.

CHAPTER NINE

JULY 24 – 30
OAKSVILLE, ONTARIO

The noted Glen Abbey Golf Club in the Toronto suburb of Oaksville was the setting of the next PGA event, the RBC Canadian Open. This was the course's 28th year hosting the third oldest tournament on the PGA schedule. Only the US and British Opens have been in existence longer.

A distinguishing feature of the course is the "Valley Holes", numbered 11 through 15. On number 11, a par four, players tee off a cliff to a fairway that is approximately 60 feet below on the valley floor. The second shot must clear Sixteen Mile Creek to the green. Holes 12, 13 and 14 all use the creek as a hazard of one form or another. Number 15 is a short par three with a sharply-sloped green, after which players climb out of the valley to the 16th hole.

The 18th is notable due to its connection to Tiger Woods, who in the final round of the 2000 Canadian open, hit a six iron shot 218 yards from a bunker on the right side of the fairway to about 18 feet from the hole. The shot was all carry over a large pond that guards the green. In doing so, Woods proceeded to defeat his playing partner Grant Waite and won the tournament. The shot is regarded as one of the most spectacular of Woods' career and recent PGA Tour history.

Only two players, Lee Trevino and Woods, have won this event and the two other national opens in the same season and it is considered the most prestigious tournament never won by Jack Nicklaus.

This year there seemed to be a special buzz associated with the tournament because a host of talented Canadian players were considered to be serious contenders for the championship. These included Nick Taylor,

Graham DeLaet, Adam Hadwin and MacKenzie Hughes, a guy who was gaining a reputation as being one of the best putters on the tour.

***

Joel Dahmen had been struggling with his putting all season long and decided it was time to try something totally different. He made arrangements to meet John Graham, Director of Golf Instruction of the Webster Golf Club in Webster, New York. Graham is a full-time putting coach for players on the PGA and LPGA tours and is a two-time recipient of the Golf Digest Best in State Award. Plus, he was named western New York PGA Teacher of the Year Award in 2016.

Graham analyzed Joel's putting stroke with the help of sophisticated electronic equipment and pronounced Joel's stroke as "really good." The problem identified was Joel's inability to see the target line very well. The pair worked on that for a while and it seemed to boost Joel's confidence. Now the challenge would be taking the information and translating it to performance on the course during the pressure of tournament competition.

***

Joel's practice round with Ryan Brehm and Ryan Williams went well and Joel praised the beauty of the golf course. Pairings were announced and Joel would be playing the first two rounds with Jonathan Randolph and Daniel Kim, an amateur playing on a sponsor's exemption. Interestingly, Geno was once again rooming with Danny Renneisen but this time they were joined by Randolph's caddie, Dave Dubord.

The first round had a lightning delay but that didn't hamper the play of Hudson Swafford, Brandon Hagy, Kevin Chappell or Matt Every, all of whom posted seven under par 65's.

Joel Dahmen struggled again and Geno described it. "His score today was much worse than he played. He hit his driver just a little wayward and had to chip out of the rough five times. That just doesn't happen. This coupled with a water ball and a couple of short missed putts and you get a 75. He is so good and is going to be good going forward. This stretch has definitely sucked but I still have faith in my man."

The 75 made making the cut highly unlikely. Playing companion Randolph also struggled and posted a 76 while amateur Kim had a 73.

There was no second round rally for anyone in the threesome as all had difficulty and did indeed miss the cut of four under par. Joel ended up four over, Randolph was plus six and Kim shot one over.

***

Joel and Geno were at wit's end and didn't know what to do about Joel's game. Joel referred to himself as Ranger Rick because his driving range practice sessions were close to perfect. He usually hit shot after shot right at the target with a slight draw and his swing felt great. On the range and in practice rounds he was terrific and almost always impressed his playing companions with his ball striking prowess. His practice partners and their caddies couldn't believe he wasn't a consistent top twenty finisher.

Practice rounds were often played with secure top 125 players Nick Taylor and Mackenzie Hughes and Joel almost always held his own with them.

So, Joel was a golfing machine Monday through Wednesday but when the bell went off on Thursday the ball started going crooked. This was puzzling because Joel said he didn't feel nervous and his swing felt free and natural. Despite feeling okay, the results were anything but. Joel was missing cut after cut and sometimes by a lot of strokes. The pattern in recent weeks was almost eerie in its similarity.

The first eighteen holes would be very poor and he often was not only out of contention but realistically over the cut line too. Then, on Friday's back nine when he was hopelessly above the cut line he would turn it on and make birdies. Geno joked "Joel, you might have the best Friday back nine scoring record on the Tour."

The frustration was increasing because there was no question about Joel's natural talent and he had full awareness of his problem. What to do about it was the big question and right now Joel didn't have an answer.

Swing coach Rob Rashell had suggested fatigue was the major cause for the slump but Bonnalie wasn't buying that. 'I have all the respect in the world for Rob but Joel says he is feeling good and we have only been competing two rounds a week. I think we have plenty of energy. We've just got to perform on tournament days."

***

WINNER'S CIRCLE – Winning a golf tournament two years in a row is unusual but Jhonattan Vegas did just that. Charley Hoffman had been the 54 hole leader at 17 under par but Vegas posted an impressive 65 on Sunday to tie Hoffman at 21 under. Then he made a birdie four on the first playoff hole to claim his third career PGA title.

A native Venezuelan, Vega had played college golf at the University of Texas before turning pro in 2008. In 2011 he got his PGA card and soon after won the Bob Hope Classic.

CHAPTER TEN

RENO, NEVADA
AUGUST 2 – 7

After eight solid weeks in the east and feeling a bit weary, Joel, Lona and Geno headed west and landed in Reno, Nevada to play in the Barracuda Championship held at the Montreux Country Club. Originally founded in 1999 as the Reno – Tahoe Open, the tournament is considered another "minor" on the PGA schedule as it is played at the same time as World Golf Championship in Akron, Ohio and therefore does not attract any of the top ranked players. FedEx points and the prize pot are about half of the normal amounts. The winner will get the two-year exemption but no invitation to the Masters.

Still, there were some players of note in the field who were trying to break into the magic top 125 in the FedEx standings and were not invited to the Akron World Golf Championship event. Included were: Aaron Baddeley, Hunter Mahan, Angel Cabrera, Stuart Appleby, KJ Choi, Davis Love III, Retief Goosen and Padraig Harrington.

The tournament is a bit unique in that it uses a modified Stableford scoring system which awards per hole points to the players as follows:

8 for an albatross (three under and rarely seen)
5 for an eagle
2 for a birdie
0 for a par
-1 for a bogey
-3 for double bogey or worse

The week was likely to have a bit of a party atmosphere consistent with the area itself. Gambling is legal in Nevada and both Reno and Lake Tahoe have big time casinos and the entertainment that goes with them. Also, Tahoe itself is a beautiful area with numerous options for a family.

Lona Skutt has family close to Reno and Joel's dad Ed and his wife Deb were meeting them there. Also, many friends from the Lewis-Clark Valley would be showing up to enjoy the area and be part of the tournament excitement.

Geno would also be welcoming his mom and dad Jim and JoAnne, and a Lewis-Clark delegation including golfing buddies Jason Emery, Gabe Alexander, Brian King and Jason Speck to name a few. In addition, Bob Yosaitis and wife Leinani had made the drive up from their home in Las Vegas. More important Holly and Hudson Bonnalie were meeting Geno and Hudson was going to get his first chance to watch his dad work a golf tournament. It was shaping up to be a comfortable week with familiar, supportive people in a beautiful area.

In addition, Joel and Geno had the following week off and some much needed rest was in the works. It was shaping up to be two good weeks for the weary road warriors.

***

Joel and his playing companions had the last tee time of the day on Thursday but it didn't keep Joel from having a solid round. His six birdies and two bogies gave him a 68 which translated to 10 modified Stableford points and a tie for 22nd. Leader John Huh had 15 points which was one better than Appleby and Miguel Angel Carballo.

Playing the back nine first, Joel got off to a good start on the tenth hole by hitting a wedge to four feet and converting the putt for a birdie three. He was close to the green in two on the par five 13th and got the ball up and down for birdie, then holed a seventeen foot putt for another birdie on 15. He hit his second shot on the par five 18th in the water and had to settle for bogey to card a 34.

The front nine was very similar. On number two he hit a wedge to eight feet for birdie, and on the 5th he flagged an iron from 168 yards and converted a short putt for another one. He bogeyed the 7th but finished strong with a 10 foot birdie on the ninth for another 34.

The playing companions didn't fare as well. Bobby Wyatt, a fellow rookie from the Web.com who finished just a couple positions in front of Joel in the Web rankings, earned only one Stableford point. Meanwhile, Tom Morton a teaching pro from Sacramento who got in the field by winning a Northern California Golf Association qualifying event, triple bogeyed his last two holes and was last in the field with minus 11 points.

By the time Joel got home, cleaned up and had dinner, it was almost time to go to bed because he had a quick turn-around for round two. The 9:00 time gave him very little time to recharge himself. It didn't matter. He handled it very well.

The front nine on Friday was solid if not spectacular. He had eight pars and a birdie on the par five second to shoot 35 and gain two Stableford points. The back nine was also bogey-free but he made four birdies for a 32 and a day long total of 10 points. This gave Joel 20 at the tournament's midpoint good for a tie for eighth.

With dusk rapidly approaching and the course almost empty, Ricky Werenski eagled the 18th hole to grab the tournament lead with 26 points. Werenski, like Joel a rookie from the Web.com Tour, needed a strong finish because he was currently ranked 154th in FedEx points so he was in position to crack the top 125. Appleby was second with 24 points and in third with 23 were veteran Dicky Pride, Ben Martin, Greg Owen and Luke List. Pride's play was impressive. He is 48 years-old and has one PGA victory which was the St. Jude twenty three years ago!

Joel's four birdies on the closing nine holes were impressive. On number 13, he almost reached the par five in two and got it up and down from the greenside bunker to get his rally going. He followed that up with a wedge to five feet on the 14th and dropped the putt. On the 207 yard par three 16th, he laced his iron to 13 feet and made that putt as well. Finally, he closed the round with two spectacular shots on the long par five 18th hole. After a 333 yard drive, he knocked his second shot 257 yards to the middle of the green and easily two-putted for the day's ending birdie.

***

Friday night was a great time for Joel, Geno and their family and friends. Joel was playing well and everyone was in a festive mood and having fun. After some tough previous weeks, Joel was in a great spirits and was looking forward to the weekend.

"It was so fun to be playing well in front of family and old friends. Looking at my gallery and seeing my dad and guys from Lewiston I have played with forever was a kick in the butt and major high for me! In some ways, it was like old times and the support and cheers were so welcome. It was the most fun I have had on the golf course for a very long time," Joel said.

"There is no feeling quite like performing well in front of people rooting for you. I was feeling blessed and very excited," he added.

***

Holly Bonnalie was nervous about taking four-year old Hudson to the golf course for the first time but decided to bite the bullet and give it a try. Joel and Geno started on the hilly back nine on Thursday and Holly took Hudson to the caddie tent where he played with little stuffed animals. They joined the players for the front nine which was flat and easier to walk.

"He did great except on one hole he fell down and scraped his knee right when Joel was getting ready to putt. I was horrified, picked Hudson up and tried to run with him in the opposite direction so that his screams weren't quite so loud. Afterwards, I mouthed 'I'm so sorry' to Joel and Geno and they both said no worries, it was fine," Holly said.

"The next day he did super on the front and then my-mother-in-law took him to the hotel so I could watch the back nine in peace. It was great," Holly added.

***

Joel hadn't seen the third round in a tournament for several weeks so he was pumped up and ready to go. Plus, he had plenty of support from family members and several hometown friends from the Lewis-Clark Valley would still be in the gallery. Unfortunately, things went sideways. Literally and in a hurry.

He started out hitting the ball pretty well but was frustrated because he had made only two birdies through thirteen holes and was slowly but surely slipping down the leaderboard. He was bogey free at this point but knew others players were making multiple birdies so he was falling way out of contention. He was especially frustrated that he hadn't been able to birdie the 13th hole which is a par five Joel had been reaching with a drive and mid iron.

So, player and caddie were not in a great mood when they stepped to the next tee. The fourteenth hole was a drivable par four because the tee had been moved up to encourage the players to gamble a bit. Joel and Geno had agreed the way to play the hole was to hit driver off the tee. This was a bit too much club for Joel because the pin was in the front portion of the green but going over eliminated all trouble and left a simple bump and run pitch shot and a likely tap-in birdie.

There was a slight tail wind on the hole and Geno urged Joel to hit a three wood instead of the driver. His thought was a good three wood could result in an eagle opportunity. Joel disagreed and wanted to stay with the driver and they kept on discussing it. Geno rarely prevails in these arguments because the ultimate decision-making lies with the player himself. But, this time Joel grumbled "you're probably" right and grabbed the three wood. But, he was not totally committed to the decision and ended up hitting his ball into a right side water hazard resulting in a penalty stroke and a bogey on the hole.

"Joel was hot! I've never seen him that mad," said Yosaitis. "He was furious at Geno who had become the focus of his anger over the poor shot," Yosaitis added.

Joel admitted being totally unnerved by the shot and said he was furious with Geno at the time. "I was actually mad at myself and when I calmed down I knew I should not have taken my frustration out on Geno. He was doing his job and I was wrong. But, I was so upset I didn't handle it well at all," Joel said frankly.

That was the start of a troubling finish. On 17, Joel who had not yet came close to regaining his poise, hit a drive into the native area which led to another penalty and double bogey 6. Then on 18, he hit another wayward tee shot and then hit his fourth shot in the water to the right of the green. The end result was Joel lost seven Stableford points on the closing holes and dropped 40 places in the tournament standings.

"Saturday night was a real downer. The high from the night before was long gone and then some. I was not fit to be around. I cancelled my dinner plans with Bob and Leinani went home to sulk," Joel said. "The other time I felt this bad was after the Web.com championship the year before when I thought I had lost my chance to earn my PGA card," Joel added.

Meanwhile, Greg Owen was playing perfect golf and was running away from the field until the final hole when he too found trouble and made a double bogey plus resulting in losing three points. Still, he entered the final round with a comfortable five point lead.

***

Joel's problems continued on Sunday and he shot the worst round of anyone in the field losing five points. This left him in 68th place and he ended up with a check of $6700.

***

WINNER'S CIRCLE – Perhaps other tournaments should consider using the modified Stableford scoring method. It can lead to some exciting finishes and it certainly did just that during Sunday's closing round.

Veteran Chris Stroud started the day in 21st position but scored an eye-popping 20 points and grabbed the clubhouse lead with 44 points. Still, there were six threesomes behind him and several players went to the reachable par five 18th hole with a chance to pass him with an eagle. This was no long-shot possibility either as the hole had yielded fifteen eagles during the first three rounds and the pin was in an easy position on the front of the green. As a matter of fact, Stroud himself had closed his round with an eagle on the hole.

Derek Fathauer, Robert Garrigus, Stuart Appleby, Tom Hoge, second round leader Richy Werenski and third round leader Greg Owen all could have won the tournament with an eagle. Werenski and Owen did birdie the hole though and both tied Stroud to force a three-man playoff.

The playoff participants assured there would be another first time winner on the PGA Tour this season. In fact, Stroud had made 284 starts on the tour without a victory and Owen was close behind with 269.

The trio went back to the 18th for the playoff and Owen was eliminated when he hit his second shot in the greenside bunker and couldn't get it up and down for a birdie to tie Werenski and Stroud. They returned to the tee and this time Werenski couldn't make the birdie needed to tie so Stroud claimed the long awaited victory.

CHAPTER ELEVEN

AUGUST 7 – 13
SCOTTSDALE, ARIZONA
LEWISTON, IDAHO

After seven straight weeks on the road, Joel Dahmen was able to return to his home in Scottsdale and Geno Bonnalie headed to Lewiston. A well-earned rest was in order for both men.

For Joel, this could not have come at a better time. He was totally beat mentally and physically. This had been compounded by the results of the past weekend which had seen him go from the top of the world to the pits in a twenty-four hour period. The happenings in Reno had truly shaken him and smashed his emotions.

On Friday night and firmly in contention to win a golf tournament, he had been surrounded by friends and family who were all upbeat and excited about his standing in the event. It was a dream come true for him. He was on the PGA Tour and performing like the great player he had always wanted to be.

Then boom. Once again golf proved it could be a very cruel game. He had hit a bad shot, lost his poise and quickly dropped to the bottom part of the leaderboard. He felt he had let his friends and family down and was embarrassed and disappointed in himself for yelling at Geno.

He made a decision that the best way to recharge was to do nothing and that's exactly what he did. His golf clubs never got unpacked, he didn't go anywhere, ordered food in, watched the PGA Championship on television, and hung out with Murphy, his black lab and couch potato buddy.

The strategy worked. He began to feel better and spent time reflecting on what he had learned over the past several weeks. The trip had not come close to producing the kind of golf results he was hoping for but it had been part of the rookie experience and thus very much worthy of analyzing.

He was unhappy that he had not been able to take his good ball striking from the driving range to the golf course when competition started on Thursday's. He was fine during practice rounds but couldn't make enough good things happen in the actual tournament. He began calling himself Ranger Rick because he was perfect on the driving range but not on the course.

This was puzzling to Joel because he was not feeling nervous or anxious during tournament play but the high scores and mistakes spoke for themselves. He decided his biggest single problem was lack of patience.

"If I make a bogey early in the round I feel I have to get it right back with a birdie. So, I press and sometimes don't play as smart as I should. There are many holes out here where par is a good score and I need to do a better job of taking them in stride and waiting for birdies to come to me," Joel said.

"This also applies to expectations. Realistically, if you are 180 yards from the hole, leaving yourself with a 25 foot putt is pretty good shot on your part. I must learn to accept that and not try to hit everything inside of six feet. I believe if I can do that, I'll be more patient and relaxed during the full course of a round," Joel explained.

So, a rested, relaxed and more reflective Joel Dahmen climbed on the airplane for the regular season final tournament in Greensboro.

As it turned out, this time off and attitude adjustment may have been the most important element of Joel's entire season. It changed the trajectory of his year and it could not have come at a better time.

***

Geno Bonnalie got in a round of golf during his break and fired a cool 67. But only one round was in the cards for him. Holly had other plans because during the nine weeks of travel, chores had piled up. Also, Hudson wanted daddy's attention and Geno was more than happy to "hang with my little man."

So, Geno was happy to be home but by week's end he was anxious to get back and hopefully earn some good money at the Wyndham. Also, this was going to be a good trip because he would only be gone one week.

CHAPTER TWELVE

AUGUST 14 – 21
GREENSBORO, NORTH CAROLINA

Mr. McIlroy,

    I would like to formally apply for the position of being your full-time caddie. I currently work for Tour Pro Joel Dahmen and have been with him for three years. I've helped lead Joel to a solo 68th finish at the Reno-Tahoe Open, T80 MDF in Puerto Rico, and also helped him make four consecutive birdies in the Sanderson Farms Championship. Please don't think I'm sneaking around behind Joel's back trying to get another job. I think Joel himself may also be applying for the position.

    If you hire me it wouldn't be awkward at all because we already know each other. We played in front of you on Saturday at the Travelers and during the wait on 4 tee box I asked you if you wanted water (which you politely declined). So, we're pretty much best friends already.

    Things that I excel at as a caddie:

-I'm really good with numbers….especially at elevation. What? You want me to take 2% of 157 yards….BAM 154. (Do you want decimal points? I know you're good but Joel and I usually work in whole yards.)

-I'm ALWAYS on time. In fact, I'm always early. I'm typing this on my way to Wyndham where I am 3 hours early at the airport.

-I am an EXCELLENT bunker raker. In fact, I would say I'm one of the best in the world. If they had bunker raking contests on tour, I would lead in every possible statistic.

-Once upon a time I was one of the best archers in the world (as a youth). So, I have a weird ability to know exactly how far you are from the pin just by looking at it (inside 70 yards). So, if I don't step anything off, and tell you it's 58 yards....it's 58 yards.

    -During practice rounds I like making bets on various shots. Joel and I have a running $5 bet on any given shot, and then give odds with the degree of difficulty. I've made an extra $370 this year betting on 3 footers. It's a nice little supplemental income.

    Things I request from you as a player:

    -If we both read a putt to go left and it doesn't go left. Please don't yell at me. It's not like I was trying to sabotage you.
-If we agree on a club, then you chunk the sh** out of it and yell are me for "giving you a bad club" I'll probably eat it and say "sorry pro", but please know that in my head I will be thinking something about how you should hit a better shot.
-if it's our first time playing a course, and you hit one 175 yards off line and immediately ask me "what's over there" odds are I have no idea.

    My shortcomings as a caddie:

    -if you make me keep our playing partners score, I sometimes lose track of what they made on a hole because I'm so focused on what we're doing (see what I did there? Turned a negative in to a positive)
-I'm not sure if I'm any good at tending the pin. In the 3 years I've been caddying, I've never once tended one. Joel just has me pull it. He says if he can't see the hole, what are the chances of making it anyway. He kind of knows where it's at.
    Anyway you probably have a lot of follow up questions you'd like to ask me. Go ahead and have your agent get a hold of my agent and I'm sure we can figure something out.

    The above was a tweet Geno Bonnalie composed on an airplane on his way to North Carolina and he did, indeed cc Rory McIlroy who several weeks before had announced he would be looking for a new caddie. The tweet was picked up by producers of the Golf Channel and it was publicized on GC's web site and reproduced a number of times on Facebook and other social media platforms. It once again highlighted Geno's happy go lucky and humorous side and nobody got more of a laugh than Joel Dahmen.

***

The letter was just the beginning of a couple of enjoyable days for Geno. First, there was no "Lewiston flightmare". He caught an inexpensive flight from Spokane to Chicago and then a non-stop directly to Greensboro. Also, he was once again staying with three other caddies but this time it was in a four bedroom house instead of a hotel room meant for two.

Also, there was a special caddie tent at the course that served a full complimentary lunch every day and had full juice bar to boot. Plus, Barbasol put on a first-class cocktail party and dinner that attracted over 100 tour caddies at the Chop House, one of Greensboro's very best restaurants. As a further perk Barbasol gave everyone there a $50 gift card for another meal at the Chop House.

"Greensboro is my favorite tour stop by far. Caddies never get this kind of royal treatment at other venues. They spoiled us," Geno said happily.

The golf was good too. On Tuesday, Joel played a practice round with Nick Taylor and took a bit of cash from him by playing very well. Then on Wednesday, Joel and Geno took some cash from Ryan Brehm and his caddie in a round where Geno made seven birdies on his own ball.

So, life was good in Greensboro except for one thing. The heat and humidity were stifling and it was close to impossible to stay fully hydrated. The week was going to demand the consumption of loads of water for player and caddie alike. This is the story of summer golf in the south and part of the lessons learned by rookies on the PGA Tour.

There was also a rather strange thing Geno saw on Monday. He almost always walks the course on Mondays to check yardages and make notes that are used to determine playing strategies, club selection, etc. once the tournament begins on Thursday. These notes also become important talking points during Tuesday's practice round.

Many tournaments have pro-am events on Mondays and Wednesdays but only the more established professionals are invited to participate in them. This was the case in Greensboro so Geno would often stop his walk to avoid bothering players about to hit a shot. On the fifteenth hole, he noticed a huge logjam around the green and someone explained what had happened.

A member of the group on the green waved the group on the fairway to go ahead and hit their second shots to the green. James Hahn thought this was unusual but complied and hit his shot. To his horror, Hahn saw that nobody on the green was watching his ball flight and he yelled fore as loud as he could. But, the ball struck an amateur's caddie square in the middle of the head and knocked him out cold.

Hahn felt terrible but everyone involved said it was not his fault. The guy on the green had not told any of his group that he had waved the group behind up so they did not know Hahn was hitting. Anyway, Geno jumped in and helped by carrying the amateur's bag the rest of the way while the caddie received medical attention.

***

The immortal Sam Snead's name is synonymous with golf in the greater Greensboro area. He won the greater Greensboro Open eight times including 1965 when he became the oldest player to win a PGA Tour event.

The Greater Greensboro Open was first played in 1938 and became the Wyndham Championship when Wyndham took over sponsorship in 2007. In addition to Mr. Snead's influence, the tournament carries another point of significance. Charles Sifford competed here in 1961 and became the first African-American to play as a professional in a tournament held in the southern United States.

The tournament is also very special to a bunch of players grouped around the magic 125 mark in FedEx Cup standings. It is the last regular event of the PGA season so it is the last chance for many players to crawl into the top 125 which carries a full exemption to next year's tour and a chance to compete in the multi-million dollar FedEx Cup playoffs.

One of the most interested participants was Richy Werenski who had been in a playoff the week before in Reno. Werenski lost in the playoffs but earned enough points to get in the 122nd spot for the season. He and Brandon Hagy, who was safe in position number 106, were paired with Joel for the first two rounds of the tournament.

***

Joel made six birdies and three bogeys in round one for a 67. Werenski also had 67 which left them six shots behind first round leader Matt Every who lit it up with an impressive 61. Hagy never got it going and finished with an uninspiring 70.

For a while it looked like Joel was going to make a major move up the leaderboard in the second round. Starting on the tenth hole, he birdied 10, 14, 15 and 18 for a very good 31 on his front nine. Then he kept it going with another birdie when he reached the par five fifth hole in two shots. At this point he was bogey free, 8 under for the tournament, and in a tie for ninth place with three holes left. Unfortunately, he finished poorly with a bogey on the seventh and a double on the ninth. This left him at five under par and tied for 37th place.

Werenski did what he needed to do. He shot 66 and was in a tie for 19th. His top 125 FedEx finish was secure at this point. After watching him for two days, Geno Bonnalie was very impressed with "a pure putting stroke." "He knocked in a mile worth of putts. He was incredible to watch," Geno marveled.

Hagy had another 70 and missed the minus three cut line by three shots.

First round leader Every didn't have it in round two and slipped back in a tie with Werenski. Meanwhile, Ryan Armour and veteran Webb Simpson became co-leaders at 13 under par.

***

Henrik Stenson roared to the front of the pack after round three and sat at 16 under par heading to Sunday's final round. Kevin Na and Ollie Schniederjans joined Simpson at 15 under so the stage was set for a close finish. Werenski kept it going with a solid 64 and was only three shots back in sixth place.

Joel was paired with Bud Cauley for the third round and the players moved in different directions. Joel shot 72 and tumbled from T35 to T62. Cauley improved his position with a 68 and sat T29 heading to Sunday.

Then on Sunday once again it was a story of players moving in opposite directions but this time it was Joel who headed the right way. His closing round 66 moved him up twenty spots and he ended up cashing a check for $18,662. Playing partner Bobby Wyatt's 74 pushed him to the very bottom of those who got to play Sunday and he settled for $5800.

A good closing round is always a positive thing but this time it might have meant just a bit more for Joel. It had been a while since he had a good finish and he needed it to build momentum for the upcoming Web.com playoffs.

***

WINNER'S CIRCLE – 41 year-old Swedish player Stenson outgunned Schniederjans down the stretch to claim a one-stroke victory, his sixth PGA Tour championship. The two kept draining birdie putts on the back nine and left the rest of the field in their wake with their spectacular play.

The long hitting Stenson left his driver in the locker room all week and certainly didn't need it as he worked his way around the Sedgefield Club setting a new tournament record of 22 under par.

***

FEDEX WATCH - The final round of the Wyndham was cause for great joy or grave disappointment for eight players in the field. Four golfers not in the top 125 at the start of the day moved into in by day's end while four others went from in to out.

The four successful players have full exemption status on the PGA Tour next season and gain entry into the FedEx playoffs. The other four now must compete in the Web.com playoffs and do well enough there to keep PGA playing privileges for the 2017 – 18 season.

WALKING WITH TIGERS

MOVING IN
Martin Flores started at 139, finished at 118
Rory Sabbatini started at 148, finished at 122
Harold Varner III started at 138, finished at 123
JJ Henry started at 134, finished at 124

MOVING OUT
Zach Blair started at 122, finished at 126
David Hearn started at 121, finished at 128
Seamus Power started at 123, finished at 130
Daniel Summerhays started at 124 finished at 131

PART FOUR

WALKING WITH TIGERS

THE WEB.COM PLAYOFFS

THE PLAYOFF FIELD

Adams, Blake
Albertson, Anders
Alker, Steven
Ancer, Abraham
Anderson, Mark
Appleby, Stuart
Armour, Ryan
Arnold, Jamie
Atkins, Matt
Axley, Eric
Baker, Chris
Barnes, Ricky
Beljan, Charlie
Blaauw, Jacques
Blair, Zac
Brehm, Ryan
Burgoon, Bronson
Byrd, Jonathan
Campbell, Brian
Campos, Rafael
Castro, Roberto
Cejka, Alex
Chin, John
Collins, Chad
Conners, Corey
Cook, Austin
Covello, Vince
Crane, Ben
Curran, Jon
Dahmen, Joel
Davis, Brian
Drewitt, Brett
Duke, Ken
Duncan, Tyler
Diaz, Roberto
Ernst, Derek
Etulain, Julián
Fdez-Castaño, Gonzalo
Garnett, Brice
Gibson, Rhein
Gonzales, Andres
Gooch, Talor
Gore, Jason
Griffin, Lanto
Gunn, Jimmy
Guthrie, Luke
Gutschewski, Scott
Hadley, Chesson
Harkins, Brandon
Harmon, Matt
Harrington, Scott
Hend, Scott
Hodge, Jonathan
Hoge, Tom
Hossler, Beau
Hubbard, Mark
Hueber, Justin
Ishikawa, Ryo
Jaeger, Stephan
Johnson, Michael
Jones, Matt
Kennerly, Billy
Kohles, Ben
Lamb, Rick
Landry, Andrew
Langley, Scott
Lashley, Nate
Lee, D.H.
Lee, Kyoung-Hoon
Levin, Spencer
Lindheim, Nicholas
Long, Adam
Loupe, Andrew
Lovelady, Tom
Luck, Curtis
Lunde, Bill
MacKenzie, Will
Mahan, Hunter
McCarthy, Denny
Merritt, Troy
Mitchell, Keith

Moore, Taylor
Mullinax, Trey
Muñoz, Sebastián
Norlander, Henrik
Núñez, Augusto
Oppenheim, Rob
Ortiz, Carlos
Owen, Greg
Park, Jin
Park, S.J.
Percy, Cameron
Pereira, Mito
Peterson, John
Piller, Martin
Poston, J.T.
Potter, Jr., Ted
Power, Seamus
Pride, Dicky
Prugh, Alex
Putnam, Andrew
Randolph, Jonathan
Reeves, Seth
Reifers, Kyle
Ridings, Tag
Roach, Wes
Romero, Andres
Ryder, Sam
Saunders, Sam
Schenk, Adam
Shindler, Conrad
Silverman, Ben
Skinns, David
Sloan, Roger
Southgate, Matthew
Stefani, Shawn
Stegmaier, Brett
Straka, Sepp
Summerhays, Daniel
Svensson, Adam
Teater, Josh
Thompson, Kyle
Thompson, Michael
Thompson, Nicholas
Tracy, Ethan
Tringale, Cameron
Uihlein, Peter
Wagner, Johnson
Wheatcroft, Steve
Wilcox, Willy
Wilkinson, Tim
Wittenberg, Casey
Yun, Andrew

CHAPTER ONE
THE SCENARIO

Where will Joel Dahmen and Geno Bonnalie be walking next season? Will they still be walking with the Tigers on golf's biggest stage or will they be forced to start all over by returning to the Web.com Tour? The answer will be determined by their performance in the Web.com playoffs.

Basically, the playoffs are four separate tournaments at four different sites. Each tournament has its own prize pool but the most important number by far is the final standings. This will be the player's placement based on accumulated money earnings during the four events.

There are times when clarity and simplicity are not part of the PGA narrative. An example is their description on how the structure of the playoffs determines the exact priority of PGA Tour status for the following season. It reads as follows:

Beginning in 2013, the Web.com Tour became The path to the PGA Tour by awarding all 50 cards for the following PGA Tour season.

The basic structure remains intact to this day, with the top 25 money leaders from the regular season being guaranteed PGA Tour cards for the following PGA Tour season and 25 additional cards being available through the four-tournament Web.com Tour Finals.

The field makeup of the finals is broken down as follows: the top 75 money leaders from the Web.com Tour at the end of the regular season, PGA Tour members who are 126 – 200 on the FedEx Cup points list following the Wyndham Championship (Joel Dahmen's entry as he finished 177th) and non-members who would have earned enough points to place them 126 – 200 on the official FedEx Cup points list.

A FEW NOTES REGARDING THE STRUCTURE OF THE FINALS:

1 – While the top 25 players from the Web.com Tour regular season will earn their PGA Tour cards, their order of priority won't be determined until the conclusion of the Web.com Tour finals. They will now carry their earnings into the finals and priority will be established on the combination of regular season and finals earnings.

2- Of those players from the Web.com Tour regular season, top-25 list, the number 1 player at the conclusion of the finals based on combined regular season and finals earnings will receive fully exempt status on the PGA Tour. So any top-25 player can earn the coveted number 1 position if he performs well enough in the final four events. In addition to his PGA Tour exemption, the number 1 player receives an exemption into the Players Championship for the upcoming season.

A separate money list for the Web.com Tour finals will determine the final 25 PGA Tour cards. The player who earns the most money during the four final events (excluding the first 25 from the regular season) will earn fully exempt status on the PGA Tour plus an invitation to the Players.

Also note, any player who is number 1 to 25 on the Web.com Tour regular season money list as of the regular season final event who earns enough money solely as a result of his play in the Web.com Tour finals events such that he would have been number 1 on the Web.com Tour finals money list shall be placed in the number 1 position on that list and shall be entitled to the benefits of that position. In such case, such player's other position on the number 1 to 25 regular season and finals combined money list shall be skipped and the order of players shall continue as identified above. In such case, the leading 25 players from the Web.com Tour finals money list will still earn their PGA Tour card.

3 – The ordering of all 50 players after the Web.com Tour finals will be done on an alternating basis, with the top position going to the number 1 player from the combined regular season and finals money list and the second position going to the leading money winner from the four Web.com Tour finals. The sequence then alternates between the combined regular season and finals money list (Nos. 3, 5, 7, 9, etc) and the Web.com Tour finals money list (Nos. 4, 6, 8, 10, etc.) through the 25th player on both lists.

***

Translation – If Joel plays well he will keep his PGA Tour privileges for next season and, if he doesn't, he won't. When the haze clears, he needs to play well enough in the playoffs to beat five out of every six players involved.

Brad Yosaitis, Bob's son and Joel's friend, had done some research and found that anyone who had a top-six finish or better in any single event had gotten their card for the following season. A couple of top 15 finishes would secure a spot as well. In the past, the magic dollar number has been $36,000.

Joel seemed confident going into the playoffs and said he was both optimistic and enthused. "I have known for a couple of months that, barring a miracle, I was going to be playing in the playoffs and I'm actually excited to do well and upgrade my ranking going into next season. There are other guys like Ricky Barnes who has had his card for fifteen years or so and he and those like him are probably dreading this," Joel reasoned. "For guys like me, it's just part of the growing process," he added.

★

Last season Joel qualified for the PGA Tour by wrapping up the 25th and final spot on the season-long Web.com money list. He didn't get to improve his position though because he couldn't participate in the playoffs due to his hand injury.

He had not been assured of getting that last spot until the final putt had been struck in the final round of the Winco, the Web.com Tour Championship held at Pumpkin Ridge near Portland, Oregon. Joel had missed the cut in that event and could have been bumped from his spot if Jack Maguire birdied the 18th hole. But Maguire missed the birdie putt and Joel was safe.

This year, the Winco produced the same kind of drama and the scenario was so similar to the previous year that it was almost eerie. Roberto Diaz sat in the 25th spot but had missed the cut and could do nothing but watch as others determined his fate. It finally came down to Keith Mitchell who was playing in the final group on Sunday and needed to birdie either 17 or 18 to wrestle the 25th spot from Diaz.

On the par three 17th, Mitchell hit a solid six iron to about 18 feet and left the birdie putt on the lip so it all came down to the final hole, on the final day, by the player in the final group. It was exactly the same situation as last year.

Mitchell bombed his drive on the par five 18th and had a mid-iron left to the green. But, he pulled his second shot left and had to get the ball up and down to get the coveted card. He hit his chip a bit past the pin but had a very makeable putt. Unfortunately for him, he pushed it a little and Diaz kept his spot.

All of this points to how fickle life can be in the world of professional golf. Mitchell and Diaz had played all year long, at all kinds of venues, in all kinds of conditions yet, in the end, it came down to one final putt. This was exactly the same as it had been for Joel Dahmen in the previous year.

And, what did Joel's holding on to the 25th spot mean in practical terms? Joel spent the year on the PGA Tour and, though he finished 171st on the money list, he still cashed checks totaling $344,824. Maguire struggled on the Web.com Tour and won $49,311 which was not enough to earn him a spot in this year's playoffs. His golf season was over with no chance of advancing to the PGA.

CHAPTER TWO
FALLEN TIGERS

During the history of the PGA there have been dozens of examples of highly ranked and respected players who suddenly lost their golf games and soon after, their Tour playing privileges.

There are five such players in this year's Web.com playoffs but none is more striking than Hunter Mahan. He was certainly one of the biggest Tigers on the planet and rose to the lofty number four spot in the world rankings.

He was a six-time winner on the Tour and had accumulated an eye-popping $30,000,000 in career earnings. He was on seven Ryder and President's Cup teams and had commercial opportunities galore.

Today he is 791st in the world rankings and is struggling to play well enough in the playoffs to retain playing privileges in 2017 – 2018.

Stuart Appleby is also trying to win back his card in the playoffs as are Ben Crane, Jonathan Byrd and Ricky Barnes. The veteran Appleby started his career in his home country of Australia and has 11 professional wins, 9 of which are PGA victories. He has won over $29,000,000 on the Tour and has been chosen for five President Cup teams. Today he is 494th in the world ranking.

Crane has had his PGA card since 2002 and now he is trying to keep it for a sixteenth season via the playoffs. He has $20,000,000 in money won and has five PGA wins on his resume. Today he is 364th in the world rankings.

Crane and Mahan are two of the four members of the "Golf Boys", a rock band that also includes Bubba Watson and Rickie Fowler. Their musical prowess is unknown but it is safe to say they are the most talented golfing band in the world.

The thirty-nine year old Byrd turned professional in 2000 and quickly made his mark by being the PGA's Rookie of the Year in 2002. He had star written all over him and won five PGA events and over 18 million dollars before losing his card two years before.

Barnes was not as accomplished as the other four but he does have $8,000,000 in career money and defeated Mahan to win the US Amateur in 2002.

The stories of these five former Tigers once again points to the extreme difficulty of keeping a PGA card and highlights the intensity of the Web playoffs.

CHAPTER THREE
PREPARATION

AUGUST 21 – 28
SCOTTSDALE, ARIZONA

Joel and Geno returned to their homes for another week off prior to the playoff opener. Joel worked with swing coach Rob Rashell on Wednesday in a "tune-up" session. Mechanics were not discussed but there was special emphasis placed on Joel maintaining his club head speed through three-quarter and punch shots. Then, Dahmen and Rashell joined another couple of good local players for a round on Thursday morning. This proved to be especially helpful because Rashell was able to observe Joel both on and off the course in a period of less than 24 hours and pronounced him "ready to go."

"I feel great about where he is at mentally and physically. We talked a lot about his approach and preparation and I'm anticipating a very good result. His swing is so good he just has to relax and let things happen and I think he will," Rashell said.

Joel was feeling good and had made a vow that, no matter what, he would stay positive. At times this season, he had been plagued by negative thinking especially after a bad shot or two and sometimes this had led to a sequence of bad play that had cost him further strokes. He promised himself that he would avoid this and he and Geno discussed it at some length. Geno was more than supportive and both agreed it would likely make their closing month of the season more fun if nothing else. So, the two old friends were definitely on the same page mentally.

In addition, they would be staying at the same house as guests of John Masdea who was the father-in-law of one of Joel's best friends from the

Canadian Tour days. Joining them would be Brandon Harkins.

Masdea turned out to be a bit of a character. He was an elderly widower who lived by himself and was spry and active. But, he did have some memory issues and could not remember names or why his guests were in town. He also asked them every morning when they would be leaving and commented "you guys must really love golf. You go out there all day, every day even when it rains."

Geno said "John was a great guy who made a mean pot of spaghetti but we left a day early and got a motel room. He was tired of us and I can't blame him. Having company for that long can be a drag for someone pretty set in their ways."

Geno had spent his week off with Holly and Hudson in Lewiston and then was able to join some friends on Saturday for his annual fantasy football draft. Better yet, he was able to get in a practice round of golf at Jug Mountain in McCall, Idaho where he would be competing for a spot in the US Mid-Amateur in a couple of weeks.

Now it was time to go to work.

CHAPTER FOUR

COLUMBUS, OHIO
AUGUST 28 – SEPTEMBER 3

The first Web.com Tour playoff event was the Nationwide Children's Hospital Charity Championship held at Ohio State University's iconic Scarlet Course in Upper Arlington, a suburb of Columbus, Ohio. The course and its shorter, easier companion the Gray Course, were designed by world renowned architect Dr. Alister MacKenzie. The Scarlet Course opened in 1938 and has been the host to numerous collegiate championships, US Open qualifying and top amateur tournaments. It became a stop on the Web.com Tour in 2013.

In 2005 – 06 the Scarlet Course went through a major renovation that was supervised by none other than Columbus' favorite son and Ohio State alumni, Jack Nicklaus. It is known as a "ball striker's" course because it is quite narrow and demanding. This plays well into Joel Dahmen's strength because he is well above average in PGA driving statistics.

Also, Joel knows the course because he played it on the tour stop of the 2015 Web.com. As a matter of fact, there are three stories associated with his last visit there.

In the 2015 event, he had made the 36-hole cut but had a very poor third round and sat last in the field heading to Sunday's final. As things worked out, he was first off the tee and, for the only time in his professional career, he had no playing companion. He decided to make the most of the opportunity and have a little fun by seeing how fast he could play while still trying to post a good score. He forgot what he shot that day but remembered he did it in one hour and fifty-six minutes.

Second, it was in the Pro-Am of the 2015 when NASCAR driver Danica Patrick embarrassed Geno Bonnalie by saying "Geno, quit admiring my ass" as she was preparing to take a swing.

Third, it was also at this tournament that Joel accidently took a huge swig of his own urine after relieving himself in an empty bottle a few days prior when he and Geno were caught in a traffic jam.

This time around, Joel was determined to make memories of a different kind by playing solid golf and saving his PGA playing privileges.

***

On Tuesday, Joel played his usual practice round at the tournament course with Brandon Harkins, Mark Hubbard and Lanto Griffin. On Wednesday, he and Geno put in a good practice session on the range and then the two of them joined a representative from Barbasol and another from the marketing agency representing Joel for a pleasant round at Scioto Country Club.

Joel's opening round tee time was 8:47 Thursday off the tenth tee. He was paired with Steve Wheatcroft, a 39 year-old who finished 179th in the PGA FedEx standings and had been a professional for sixteen years. His best finish this season was a tie for 10th at the St. Jude but he had won two PGA titles, the last in 2004.

Rounding out the threesome was Casey Wittenberg who had finished 41st on the Web.com money list and had won a Web event in 2012.

Wheatcroft shot a one under par 70 which was five behind leader Keith Mitchell, the same guy who had missed automatically getting his PGA card by failing to birdie the last hole at Pumpkin Ridge.

Wittenberg had a 75 and Joel carded a disappointing three over par 74. He had birdied number 12 but double bogeyed the 15th to turn at one over. He got that shot back with a birdie on the fourth but once again failed to finish strong. He made three bogeys on the final five holes and was tied for 90th at day's end.

***

The weather had been near perfect in round one but turned windy for Friday's second round. Joel and Geno knew they were in danger of missing the cut and earning no money in their quest to keep the coveted PGA card.

They were right.

Dahmen made an eagle on the 6th hole but gave the two shots right back by making bogeys on the 8th and 10th holes. He rallied with solid birdies on 12 and 13 but a bogey on 15 left him squarely on the projected cut number of two over as he headed for the 18th. He hit his drive and second shots in the rough and faced a fifteen foot putt to save par. Joel knocked the putt in the dead center of the cup and that proved to be a big deal because the projected cut line stayed at plus two and he advanced to weekend play by the skin of his teeth.

Wittenberg shot another 75 and missed the cut by six strokes but Wheatcroft's second straight 70 left him at two under par in a tie for 17th place.

Mitchell continued his strong iron play with a 67 and had a two stroke lead over the field with an impressive score of 10 under par. He had obviously put the Portland disappointment behind him and was performing like someone who was going to be very difficult to beat.

***

The PGA and Web.com Tours usually pair players in twosomes for the final two rounds of tournaments but rain was predicted so they scheduled threesomes in case play needed to be suspended at some point. So, Joel was paired with Roberto Castro and Mark Hubbard for Saturday.

This was an interesting pairing. All three men were coming off the PGA Tour and all were in the playoffs for the same reason. They were in the zone of 126 – 200 in FedEx Cup points. Castro had finished 172nd and Hubbard at 189th. However, Castro and Hubbard had more experience than Joel.

Castro had been a PGA rookie in 2015 – 2016 and had easily kept his card for this season by finishing an impressive 22nd in the FedEx standings during his rookie season. He had obviously had a big fall off this year as his best finish was a tie for 20th at the Greenbrier. Still, he had successfully kept a PGA card once and was confident he would repeat.

Hubbard's record was not quite as good but still had an element of past success. He too had been a rookie in 2015 – 2016 and also kept his card by finishing 115th in the FedEx race. This season his best showing was a tie for

18th at the Barracuda tournament.

The rain had come as predicted and had softened the hard, fast greens. But, that didn't make things easier as the course, especially the rough, was wet and soggy and the rain didn't let up during the entire round.

Joel had four birdies and four bogeys and moved up a few spots with his even par 71. He sat 53rd among the 70 who had made the cut. Hubbard also moved forward a bit with a 70 but Castro's 73 put him near the bottom.

Meanwhile, Ryan Armour put on a ball-striking clinic in the wet, soggy conditions and his impressive 65 gave him the tournament lead at 12 under par. This was a shot better than Mitchell.

***

The good weather was predicted to return on Sunday so the players were put in twosomes for the final round. Joel was set to play with Mitro Pereira, a young pro from Chile who had played college golf at Texas Tech. Pereira had finished 64th on the Web money list and his best finish had been a tie for third in Nashville.

Joel knew every dollar might be important in determining his final playoff position and he was determined to move up the leaderboard with a good round. Unfortunately, the plan was derailed early when a disheartening triple bogey was made on the 7th hole. He ended up shooting 74 and dropped to 63rd. Pereira fared better with a 70 and move up a little to tie for 49th.

Joel's winnings were only $2510 so he had a lot of work to do in the final three tournaments. Next week was off and then the field would head to Boise, Idaho for the Albertson's Boise Open.

***

WINNER'S CIRCLE – Peter Uihlein had been near the lead all week long and jumped out of the pack on Sunday with a 65 to claim a one stroke victory over Ryan Armour. Armour bogeyed the last hole after hitting a poor drive, one of his very few bad shots of the entire week.

The 28 year-old Uihlein had spent the past four seasons playing primarily in Europe but he was certainly no stranger to successful golf in the United

States. He was the US Amateur champion in 2010 and was a two-time All-American during his tenure at Oklahoma State University. He had also been on a Walker Cup team.

The strong performances locked in 2017 - 2018 PGA Tour cards for both Uihlein who won $180,000 and Armour who made $108,000. Also, getting his card as result of his tie for third was long-hitting Tom Lovelady who cashed $58,000.

Andrew Landry had also made $58,000 but he had already secured his card as a top 25 finisher on the regular season money list. Abraham Ancer had also earned his card earlier but won $40,000 for finishing fifth.

And, what happened to Keith Mitchell? He faded a bit on the weekend and tied for sixth with one of the veteran fallen tigers, Ben Crane. Both won $34,750 and, if past history held true and the magic number stayed at $36,000, they could assure their cards by making one cut in the final three tournaments.

THE OTHER FALLEN TIGERS - Hunter Mahan finished in good shape. He tied for 13th and was in a strong position with winnings of $18,750. Jonathan Byrd made the cut and cashed a check for $5400, a long way from contention but certainly better than Barnes and Appleby who missed the cut.

CHAPTER FIVE
LAST WEEK OFF

SEPTEMBER 3 – 10
LEWISTON, IDAHO

The last off week of the season was a very good one for Geno Bonnalie. It started a little hectic as his flight from Columbus didn't land in Spokane until midnight and he still faced a two-hour drive to Lewiston. He grabbed a quick three hours of sleep and then he and Holly made their way to the Lewiston Golf & Country Club to participate in a one-day couple's Labor Day tournament.

Holly is a beginner and doesn't have an established handicap but this particular event is aimed at fun and maximum handicaps are often assigned to encourage participation. It features an alternate shot format that is also friendly for inexperienced golfers.

"Holly was a star today! She knocked in putts from all over the place and we won our flight," Geno exclaimed. Holly laughed and said "It's the only time I have ever done anything positive on a golf course. Think it was a fluke but it was fun!"

Another Labor Day tradition in Lewiston is the annual Sole Survivor tournament, an event that Joel Dahmen won multiple times as a teenager. It is serious golf all the way with a big gallery and ten solid players who qualified during the weekend's tournament. The ten golfers tee off on number one and one is eliminated on every hole based on high scores and chip offs. At the end, the two finalists compete for the championship.

All players have friends who caddie for them during the survivor but qualifier Brian King outdid them all by having Geno carry his bag thus having

WALKING WITH TIGERS

the only professional caddie in the field. As usual, Geno got right in the spirit of this good fun by wearing his John Deere caddie bib and pinning on a sign saying KING. This made all participants and gallery members smile and added to the festive mood.

And, to top it off, King won the event for the fourth time. He and Geno were featured the next morning in the local Lewiston Morning Tribune newspaper with two pictures and a banner headline reading - KING OF THE HILL.

***

When Geno was putting together his travel schedule for 2016 – 17 he noticed that a qualifying site for the national Mid-Amateur Tournament was scheduled in McCall, Idaho which is halfway between Lewiston and Boise, the site of the next Web.com playoff tournament.

This worked out perfectly for Joel also. He had donated a round of golf for an auction item benefitting the Lewis-Clark State golf team and it sold for $400. So, he and Lona flew into Lewiston, played the round and got in a quick family visit.

On Saturday afternoon Geno, Joel and Lona drove to McCall and PGA player and caddie switched roles for a day and Joel toted the bag during the qualifying event. Lo and behold! Geno's great week continued and he beat 22 other players to claim the site's lone qualifying spot in the Mid-Amateur finals in Atlanta.

This caused Joel to tweet: Geno's caddie is a lot better than mine!"

The final is set for the week after the last Web playoff tournament.

CHAPTER SIX

SEPTEMBER 10 – 16
BOISE, IDAHO

The second leg of the Web.com Tour Playoffs was the Albertson's Boise Open presented by Nabisco. The tournament was started as the Boise Open in 1990 and changed to the Albertson's Boise Open in 2002. The tournament has always been held at the Hillcrest Country Club and is now entrenched as a Web playoff stop.

Boise is the third largest city in the Northwest behind Seattle and Portland with an official total of 235,000 people in the city limits but nearly twice that when adding in suburbs such as Caldwell, Nampa and Meridian. It is also about a five hour drive from the Lewis-Clark Valley which makes it the closest thing to a home field as it gets for Joel who has played here since he was in junior golf.

Both Geno and Joel had friends and family attending and Joel said "I really like it here. I love the area and it feels like home to me." His dad Ed and stepmother Deb were in town as were friends Mike and Helen Henry and Jason and Deanna Speck. Holly and her dad Ron and also made the trip along with their friends Gabe and Megan Alexander. But, Joel's favorite gallery member was Geno's old fraternity brother and host Dave Judd who Joel described as "loud, fun and enthusiastic."

***

Joel's playing partners for the first two rounds were both older guys who have been golf professionals for a long time. Jin Park was born in South Korea but played golf at Arizona State University and turned professional in 2002. The

37-year old had played on the PGA Tour in 2008 and was in this year's playoffs because he finished 66th on the Web money list during the regular season.

40-year old Steven Alker is from New Zealand and he turned professional in 1995. He was 186th in PGA FedEx points this season and had been one of Joel's playing companions in Joel's first PGA tournament in Mississippi.

There is an old saying that "you can't win a golf tournament on Thursday but you can sure lose one." That appeared to apply to Joel in round one. He had one of the last tee times and was stumbling along at even par through 15 holes. On some courses that would be okay but Hillcrest gives up lots and lots of birdies and, at that exact moment, Joel was in 90th place. Then he rallied with an eagle-par-birdie finish and ended up with a respectable 68 which moved him to a tie for 37th, six shots behind the still red hot Peter Uihlein who fired a first-day leading 62.

Park also did okay and matched Joel's 68 while Alker had a solid 65.

The course played much tougher on day two because of a cold and persistent twenty-mile-per-hour wind. This was reflected on the scoreboard and in the Dahmen threesome. Joel shot a one-under par 70 to put him in a tie for 37th and two shots above the cut line of two under. Alker had a 73 which put him in a tie with Joel but Park ballooned to a 76 and missed the cut.

Meanwhile, Tyler Duncan handled the conditions beautifully with an impressive 64 and moved to the tournament lead at 12 under par. This was good for a one-shot lead over veteran Alex Cejka and Tyler Moore. First round leader Uihlein fell back into a tie for 16th after shooting a three over par 74.

***

Dahmen was paired with Austin Cook for the third round. Cook was playing with house money so to speak as he had secured his PGA card already by placing 14th on the Web's regular season money list.

Saturday is known as "moving day" in golf circles and both Joel and Cook did exactly that. Cook fired a 66 and moved all the way to 11th place and Joel's 67 put him in a tie for 19th heading into the final round.

Joel's 67 was "smooth and easy" according to Bonnalie and "solid but unspectacular" according to Joel. Either way it was bogey free. On the par five 2nd and 16th holes he hit his second shot into greenside bunkers and got both sand shots up and down for easy birdies. He also drove the par four 15th hole and two putted and hit a wedge to less than two feet for a tap in birdie at nine.

This was a badly needed and appreciated step and both player and caddie were looking forward to another upward move in the final round.

Duncan's posted a three under par 68 to increase his lead to two strokes over Jonathan Randolph who jumped over several people with a 66.

***

Under blue skies and perfect 75 degree weather the fourth round was shaping up to be a potentially big and important day for Joel Dahmen and his playing partner Wes Roach. The two had much in common.

They were tied at 8 under for the tournament and both came from the PGA Tour season on shaky ground in terms of keeping their cards. Roach had finished slightly ahead of Joel in FedEx points and both had cashed small checks in the first Web playoff stop in Columbus. Roach had tied for 41st and earned $3700, about $1200 ahead of Joel. Also, both had gotten to the PGA Tour by claiming the 25th and final spot in Web.com regular season earnings. Joel had done it in 2016 and Roach in 2015.

Now the two friendly competitors were teeing it up for one of the most important rounds of their professional careers.

Joel started out with a bang by parring the first hole then making a birdie on the second. Then disaster struck.

His drive on the par five third found the deep right hand rough and his only choice for a second shot was a low slice to get back in the fairway. But he caught the ball square in the middle of the club face and it flew dead straight and ended up out-of-bounds. By the time he was done, he had putted out for a triple bogey eight and his dream of a low round ended before it got fully started.

At this point, one of two things could have happened. A rattled Joel could have blown up and fallen far down the leaderboard. Or he could have pulled himself together and tried to salvage something positive. He chose the latter and, with Geno Bonnalie's calm demeanor helping out, Joel fought on.

He made a string of pars then knocked in a long putt on eight for birdie and followed that with a tap-in birdie on the tenth. This got him back to even for the day but a three-putt resulted in a bogey on the eleventh. Then on the 16th he hit his best shot of the week.

After a perfect drive, Joel had a seven iron left to the par five. He nailed it and ended up only seven feet away. He canned that putt for an eagle three and this got him back to one under par for the day. He stayed there with a bogey – birdie finish.

The result was not great by any means as Joel fell six places into a tie for 25th place. But, in the playoffs where every dollar counts, it was an important and gutsy comeback from what could have been a terrible day. The resulting check was $8132 for a two-event playoff total of $10,642 which put him in 36th place with two events left.

Roach shot a one over par 72 which gave him two-event winnings of $7600. This placed him in the 47th slot.

***

WINNER'S CIRCLE – For the second week in a row a competitor came out of the pack with the round of the day 65 to claim the tournament championship. In Columbus it had been Peter Uihlein. This time it was Chesson Hadley who won on the Web.com Tour for the second time this season and the fourth time in his career. This assured Hadley would be returning to the PGA Tour and, in fact, it moved him into the number one spot in combined money won during the Web regular season and playoffs.

Hadley had finished like a champion by making birdies three of his last four holes to finish at 17 under par, a stroke better than Randolph and Potter. Still, this ended up being a huge day for Randolph as he locked in his PGA card and would be returning to the Tour next year. Potter had already qualified for the Tour based on his performance in the regular season.

Also earning back a card was the veteran Cejka who had 355 PGA starts under his belt but had lost his playing privileges last season. Cejka had finished alone in fourth place.

Duncan had faded to fifth but was not unhappy because he too had won the right to move up and make his first appearance as a member of the PGA next month.

Meanwhile, using the historical $36,000 as a measuring stick, four more players moved into striking distance of getting their cards. Now making a cut in either of the final two events would seal the deal for three of them because all had earned $35,120 based on their ties for ninth. They were: Adam Svenson, Matthew Southgate and Rob Oppenheim. Keith Mitchell remained at $34,750 after missing the cut and Brett Stegmaier sat at $32,500.

FALLEN TIGERS - Tiger Hunter Mahan made $2570 which coupled with his prize money from Columbus, gave him a total of $21,520. This put him 23rd in the playoffs. So, at this point he was inside the magic "25". Despite his disqualification in this tournament, Ben Crane was still in good shape with $34,750. But, Jonathan Byrd, Stuart Appleby and Ricky Barnes missed the cut so their situations did not improve at all. This was especially bad for Appleby and Barnes because they had no playoff earnings after two events.

CHAPTER SEVEN

BEACHWOOD, OHIO
SEPTEMBER 18 – 24

The third leg of the Web.com playoffs, the DAP Championship, was held at one of the oldest and most respected courses in the United States. The Canterbury Country Club was founded in 1921 and is one of only two courses to host all five of the men's national championships that rotate sites. The US Open, PGA, US Amateur, Senior US Open and the Senior PGA have all been hosted by the club in Beachwood, Ohio, a suburb of Cleveland.

The list of players who have won championships at Canterbury reads like a who's who of past golfing Tigers. Included are Walter Hagen, Arnold Palmer, Jack Nicklaus, Mark O'Meara, Chi Chi Rodriguez, and Dave Stockton. Now the Tiger wannabees were gathering here trying to win their Tour cards or, in the case of those who have already qualified, improve their exemption status for the upcoming season.

The course is a narrow par 71 that was playing to a par 70 for this event. The members claim they have the best three finishing holes in the entire golfing world. Joel Dahmen was not about to dispute that after his practice round on Tuesday and Geno Bonnalie termed the facility as "fantastic in every respect." One thing worried Geno somewhat. "Joel hits his tee shots so well we can usually attack most courses by primarily using a driver. Here that is not going to happen. Some of the dog legs require irons or five woods from the tee and distance control is actually every bit as important as accuracy. It's a bit of a different test for us," Geno explained.

Joel and Geno had flown from Boise together and were sharing a house with competitors Lanto Griffin and Brandon Harkins. When they arrived in Cleveland late Monday night, they were told only one rental car was left, a brand new Mustang convertible. This was a sporty ride but hardly practical and their golf clubs had to be seat belted in the back. Luckily, Lona was not on this trip or someone would have needed to take a cab.

***

The Web tour leaders do something interesting during the playoffs by making first and second round pairings based on playoff money standings. That meant that Joel, ranked 36th, would be playing with two men tied for 37th. The first of these was the very familiar Steve Wheatcroft who had been paired with Joel a few times during the regular PGA campaign this season. Wheatcroft had spent the last two years competing on the PGA Tour and had been a professional since his 2001 graduation from the University of Indiana.

Adam Long, a 2010 graduate from Duke who turned professional after his final college competition, was the third member of the group. He had gotten into the finals by finishing 45th on the Web regular season money list.

So the die was cast and it was time for the third leg of the playoffs on a tough golf course with a lot at stake. At times this season, the putter has been Joel's nemesis and three putts had cost him dearly. On the first hole he three-putted, lipping out the three foot second putt and started with bogey. Later he bogeyed the par four 14th hole by hitting a weak tee shot in the trees which required a pitch out.

But on this day, the putter was Joel's friend and it helped him salvage the round. He knocked in three 25 – 30 footers for birdie on the 7th, 16th and 17th holes. This led to a solid if unspectacular 69 which put him in a tie for 28th. Long and Wheatcroft both shot one over 71's, seven behind first round leader Nicholas Lindheim's 64.

***

The next day was the Bonnalie's tenth wedding anniversary and Holly sent Joel a text saying "All I want for my anniversary is an eagle."

Joel and his group went off the tenth tee and Joel got things rolling with an excellent birdie on the 12th. He hit his tee shot a bit too long through the dogleg and ended up in the rough. But he hit a solid iron in front and the ball chased up to within seven feet then holed the putt.

On the 14th Joel hit a good drive then grooved a wedge to within an inch of the hole for another birdie. He almost birdie 15 as well but on the 16th he almost gave Holly her wish. He hit an incredible three-wood second shot 277 yards and left his eagle putt on the lip.

On 17, Joel gave a classic example of how he meant to keep the promise he had made to himself after the Reno tournament. Patience. He hit his five wood tee shot on the difficult par three in the rough and "short-sided" himself. Rather than try a heroic, low percentage shot, he calmly chopped the ball on the green and two-putted for a bogey.

He finished his first nine by holing a 20-foot putt he thought he had left short on 18 for a 32.

Sometimes a par save is as good as a birdie to bolster a player's spirits. This was the case on the first hole. Joel hit his tee shot deep in the right-hand trees and had to chop the ball out sideways to get back in the fairway. But, from 111 yards he nailed a wedge to within a foot to save par.

He then strung together a series of pars before another pushed tee shot cost him a bogey on the 8th. But, that minor blemish was soon forgotten on his last hole of the afternoon on the par five ninth. A solid drive, a 254 yard three wood and a chip in for eagle gave him a 34 for 66.

Happy anniversary, Holly!

The round shot Joel up the leaderboard into a tied for 6th and put him within striking distance of leader Matt Atkins who stood at eight under for the championship.

Wheatcroft also made a big move with a near perfect 65. He moved up a whopping 49 places into a tie for 11th. Long shot 73 and missed the cut of one-over par.

FALLEN TIGERS - Ben Crane – made the cut and, if the past magic number of $36,000 held true, he had earned back his card for next season no matter what he shoots in rounds three and four. He made enough money in the Columbus tournament so that any winnings here guaranteed him a spot in the top 25.

Hunter Mahan missed the cut and was now in a position where he had to have a high finish in next week's finals to have a chance to get his card back.

Jonathan Byrd – Missed the cut with a horrific nine-over-par performance and now would need a top six finish to have any chance of moving up next season.

Stuart Appleby – Missed his third cut in the playoffs and would need a top six next week to make it back to the tour.

Ricky Barnes – Made his first playoff cut but things were looking bleak as he has at the bottom of the pack.

***

Golf can be like a giant roller coaster at times and Joel and Geno rode that coaster in an exciting third round.

The round started beautifully with a 15 foot birdie putt on the first hole. Number two has the course's most difficult green and Joel's iron shot ended up in a bad place and he had an almost impossible downhill, sliding birdie putt. Actually, birdie was the farthest thing from Joel's mind. He was grinding to get the ball down in two for par. But, the slick hard-running putt found the center of the cup and dropped for another birdie.

He missed a short birdie putt on five but, on the par three seventh he drilled a five iron to three feet and converted the birdie. At this point he was eight under for the tournament and tied for the lead!

Feeling great, Joel went to the par five ninth and hit a perfect drive. He had 222 yards left and his second shot looked like it was all over the flag. Geno loved the shot and couldn't understand why the gallery hadn't reacted. He was expecting to see a makeable eagle putt and was disheartened to see it had landed hot and rolled through the green into the rough. From there, Joel three-putted for a disappointing par and it seemed to rattle him a bit.

Still, a three-under 32 was very good stuff indeed and he was tied for third heading to the back nine.

The tenth hole could have spelled disaster. A weak iron off the tee left Joel buried in deep rough and he pulled his next shot and ended in a water hazard. After a penalty shot, he dropped and was still 50 yards from the cup. But, Joel hit a solid pitch, made the putt and the resulting bogey caused minimal damage to the round. "That bogey save was huge with a capital H. We were looking at double or more which would have been demoralizing to say the least," Bonnalie said.

Scrambling pars were made at both eleven and twelve then Joel hit his worst drive of the tournament on 13. It hit a tree and dropped straight down and he was 360 yards from the green. He was still a 100 yards away after his second shot and settled for another bogey. It was beginning to look like the wheels had come off because Joel had not hit a fairway with a tee shot for several holes.

Sometimes a good break is needed to get one's round back on track and Joel got two of them in a row on 14 and 15. On 14, he appeared to hit a good tee shot but it ran through the fairway and once again ended up in the rough. His second shot ended up short of the green and he half skulled his chip. Luckily, it hit the flag deep center and dropped for birdie.

On 15 he was facing a downhill putt for birdie and hit it a bit too hard. But, the direction was perfect and it hit the back of the cup, popped in the air and found the bottom of the cup for yet another birdie.

A bogey on the difficult 17th and a routine par on 18 finished the roller coaster ride and when all was said and done Joel was in a four-way tie for third, two shots behind co-leaders Lindheim and Atkins.

Tomorrow he would likely get plenty of television time as he was in the second to the last group with dark horse Matt Harmon who barely crawled into the playoffs by finishing 73rd on the Web.com regular season money list.

It looked like an exciting finish was on the horizon.

***

The roller coaster ride from Saturday was not over. Not by any means.

Joel made great par saves on the first and third holes and sandwiched in a birdie on the second hole to move within a shot of the lead. He gave that shot back on the fifth hole when he hit his iron approach in a greenside bunker and couldn't get it up and down for par.

After a par on six, the Golf Channel finally caught up with Joel on the seventh tee but they did not show his shot. In a few minutes they said he had tapped-in for birdie so the shot was obviously a very good one but those at home didn't see it.

The next time Joel was on camera was his chip on eight from behind the green. The announcers mentioned it was his fourth shot on the par four and for a moment it looked like he had chipped it in the cup. Instead, it power lipped out to about nine feet and he missed the putt and ended up with a harmful double bogey.

The ninth hole is the easiest on the golf course. It is a simple par five that the players often reach in two and make birdie on a rather routine basis. Unfortunately, both Joel and his playing companion hit tee shots that went left of left. In fact, Joel's ball hit a water tower and ended up in ankle deep rough behind trees. He had no choice but to chop the ball up the 12th fairway where Keith Mitchell stopped to jokingly ask him if he had a good yardage from there. Later, Joel commented that it was the only time he had seen the 12th fairway all week.

Geno did his best to pace off the yardage from the unmarked spot and Joel got the ball on the green and two-putted to salvage a very disappointing par.

The one over 36 dropped Joel off the front page of the leaderboard and he fell further back when he bogeyed the 12th. At this point he was five shots off the lead. "I was in a bit of a fog the entire back nine and wasn't watching the scoreboard at all. I was nervous, grinding and just trying to do enough to get my card back. It was exciting but I sure wouldn't call it fun," Joel remembered.

Routine pars on 13, 14 and 15 brought him to the challenging finishing holes in a position to finish off a good tournament.

The 16th is a very good par five and Joel played it perfectly. He hit a good drive then a "pure five wood that was as good as any shot I had hit all week. I thought it was good but there was no gallery and my playing partner didn't say anything so I feared it had taken a bad bounce or something. It was a full 200 yard walk before Geno and I spotted the ball and we were very relieved," Joel said. He had fifteen feet left for eagle.

Once again, the Golf Channel didn't cover these shots but they did show the putt which ended up a bit short for a tap-in birdie.

The home viewers did get to see Joel's tee shot on the long par three seventeenth and the audio picked up his voice as the ball was in the air. He said "I chunked it, Geno." Geno disputed that and said he thought Joel's mind was numb and playing tricks on him. "It sounded like he clipped it perfectly," Geno said.

Regardless, the ball hit the green and ran to about four feet from the cup.

"I was incredibly nervous and now my hands felt like they were shaking, but somehow I got it in the hole," Joel said. He had now birdied two of the toughest holes on the course back-to-back in crunch time.

At this point, Joel stood at seven under par heading to the 18th. Chesson Hadley and Rob Oppenheim were in the clubhouse at eight under and leader Nicholas Lindheim was 10 under but was in trouble at 17. A birdie would tie the clubhouse lead but Joel's roller coaster hit one final bump.

A poor drive in the rough led to a double bogey and Joel ended up in a five way tie for sixth place.

This was not the desired finish but Geno put his arm around Joel and they walked off the green with the big mission accomplished. The finish assured Joel would be in the top twenty-five in the playoffs and therefore would be returning to the PGA Tour!

Dahmen shook his head. "It was weird. I had just double bogeyed a hole yet I had a major sense of relief. It was finally real. I wouldn't be going back to the Web.com tournament next season."

It was time to celebrate and they did. Lindheim took Joel and Geno to dinner and wine and he even picked up the tab. No balloons flew or bands played, but it was a very pleasant evening for three happy friends.

Unfortunately, at that moment the friends didn't know that one last turn of events was on the horizon. Things were not as they seemed.

***

WINNER'S CIRCLE – Lindheim had built what seemed like a comfortable two-shot lead when he birdied the16th. But, bogeys on 17 and 18 put him in a three-way playoff with Chesson Hadley and Rob Oppenheim. But, a 35 foot putt can cure a lot of ills and that's exactly what Lindheim holed on the first hole of the sudden death playoff.

This was a huge win for Lindheim and he and Oppenheim joined Hadley by wrapping up their PGA cards for the next campaign. This enabled Lindheim to return to the tour and for Oppenheim it will be his first time to walk with the Tigers lurking on the PGA. The finish also wrapped up Hadley's hold as the number one overall Web qualifier which carries a full exemption into every tour event next year. It was certainly accurate to say there were no losers in this particular playoff!

It was also a very big tournament for Joel Dahmen and a few others who played well enough to earn a return trip to the big tour. Others getting the job done were Troy Merritt, Martin Piller, Brett Stegmaier and Bronson Burgoon. Plus, three would be joining Oppenheim as first timer card holders. They were Keith Mitchell, Denny McCarthy and Corey Conners.

Ben Crane, Adam Svenson, Seamus Power and Matthew Southgate were not officially in a position to advance but were over the traditional magic number of $36,000 with one event to go.

But, the numbers do not do justice to describe Southgate's position. What happened to him was bizarre and downright cruel.

The popular Englishman was rolling along beautifully in the final round and doing exactly what he had to do to secure his card. He was playing solid and comfortable golf and had it made when he approached a short, very makeable birdie putt on the 15th hole. It looked to all present like he had made the putt. But, as the ball was nearing the cup, a giant leaf blew across the green and knocked the putt off line.

Footage of this astonishingly unlucky moment spread across social media but things got worse. Much worse. Southgate had taken the bad break pretty much in stride and had tapped-in the wayward putt for a par. This par didn't hurt Southgate's chances at all but the penalties that followed were crushing.

According to the USGA's Rule 19-1, Southgate was required to replay the putt from its original position before the leaf struck the ball. He was subsequently assessed a two-stroke penalty for not replacing the ball and another two strokes for signing an incorrect scorecard.

Though it seems impossible at this point, things got even worse. He bogeyed 17 and tripled 18 to shoot 79 and fall into 66th place.

Yes, golf can be cruel. Very cruel. And, things weren't over yet. Not for Southgate or for Joel and Geno either.

CHAPTER EIGHT

SEPTEMBER 25 – OCTOBER 1
WEB.COM CHAMPIONSHIP
ATLANTIC BEACH, FLORIDA

The 2016 Web.com Championship had been scheduled at the Atlantic Beach Country Club in the Jacksonville suburb of Atlantic Beach. It had been cancelled due to hurricane Matthew and it looked like history would repeat itself as hurricane Irma roared through Florida and flooded the streets of Jacksonville just two weeks ahead prior to the event.

But, the damage had been well-managed and the final leg of the playoffs was to go on as scheduled.

The importance of this tournament to the players cannot be overstated. For those on the bubble, their performance will be their last chance to play on the PGA Tour next season.

Included in that group were the Fallen Tigers. Of the five covered in previous chapters, only Ben Crane was in a good position to regain his card. For the rest, their backs were firmly against the wall. Projections showed Hunter Mahan would need a top 13 finish while Jonathan Byrd, Ricky Barnes and Stuart Appleby would need to finish in the top six.

For those already earning their card, it is a last chance to move up the exemption priority list. This standing will often make the difference in gaining entrance to some of the more popular PGA events.

Joel Dahmen was last year's primary example of the importance of placement in these standings. He had been 50th and last in the pecking order and had therefore gotten less tournament entries than any other PGA eligible player.

For the first time all season, Joel and Geno were playing with house money, so to speak. They knew they were headed back to the PGA tour so that pressure was off. Sure placement was important, but in the big picture of things, they could relax a little. Both player and caddie said they were going to try and have a little fun for a change.

Golf had become a bit more relaxing anyway because of Joel's increased patience and more positive outlook. Plus, he was playing well. He had made five cuts in a row and was feeling good about his game.

Lodging wise, Geno had definitely moved up in the world. He would be sharing quarters with five other caddies but they had a nice condo on the beach and four of the six would actually be able to sleep in a bed.

***

Joel Dahmen was in the afternoon block of tee times for round one which added an element of difficulty. It was over 90 degrees out and the humidity felt like it could be cut with a knife. Hydration was going to be a challenge and being comfortable was not in the cards.

Joel's playoff ranking stood at number 13 so he was in a position to make a nice move forward in exemption priority ranking. His playing partners were familiar competitors Adam Svenson, a young Canadian ranked 14th and Ireland's Seamus Power, who was in the 15th spot.

From the very start it was obvious the field of players were going to turn this tournament into a birdie fest. Sam Saunders, one of six members playing their home course, got things going that way with a first round 59 and followed that with a 66 to lead at the halfway mark at 17 under par. Jonathan Byrd was doing his part to keep his card and led the group of Fallen Tigers after 36 holes with a solid second place score of 13 under.

Saunders was not only the darling of the home crowd he also had pedigree galore. Arnold Palmer, The King, was his grandfather.

Ricky Barnes was the only other tiger with a shot after 36 holes and stood at five under though Ben Crane seemed a cinch to get his but because we was safely over the target earning of $36,000. Hunter Mahan and Appleby missed the cut so they would not be getting their card.

All of this doesn't mean the end of Mahan and the others because they will get sponsor exemptions and invitations via the category of past champions. It does mean they will not get to pick and choose when and where they will play next season and their schedules will be limited to around 14 events.

***

Joel got a triple bogey seven early in his round one and his 36 hole score of even par wasn't close to making the cut which went to four under par. Svenson also missed the cut but Power slipped in at minus 5.

These results didn't seem significant at the time as the three players were all safely over the $36,000 mark and had already made their reservations for the PGA season opener next week in Napa, California.

"I tried hard to motivate myself and play hard to improve my standing but I just couldn't get it going mentally or physically. It had been a long tiring year and I was so relieved to get my card the week before that I had a letdown. Still, I was happy and ready to start the PGA campaign," Joel shared.

BUT, IN THE WORDS OF ESPN ANALYST LEE CORSO – "NOT SO FAST, MY FRIENDS!"

***

Saturday's third round was pretty routine for most players though Byrd made a huge move for the tournament and his future with a 64 and the leading 54-hole score of minus 20. Saunders closed at minus 18 a mark tied by a hard-charging Shawn Stefani.

On Sunday the rains came and the players were unable to finish the tournament. This meant the end was postponed until Monday which wreaked havoc and turned things upside down.

CHAPTER NINE

MONDAY, October 2, 2017
ATLANTIC BEACH, FLORIDA
OAKLAND, CALIFORNIA
LEWISTON, IDAHO

"IT AIN'T OVER TILL IT'S OVER" - YOGI BERRA

Oakland, California - Joel Dahmen and Lona Skutt had flown into Oakland on Saturday to spend time with a friend for a couple of days before making the short drive to Napa for the season opener of the PGA season. He was looking forward to having dinner with buddy Nick Taylor and the two were setup for a practice round on Tuesday.

His time in Oakland had been fun and relaxing and he was in high spirits when he looked at his phone to see how some of his friends were faring in the last round of the Web.com Tour playoffs. He immediately got a shock. He had fallen all the way to 25th on the projected finals list and a few people who could drop him even further back were still on the golf course 3000 miles away.

On Sunday, the Web Tour officials had decided to finish the Tour Championship on Monday rather than shorten it to a 54-hole event. This decision caused 13 players to withdraw and almost all of them were people who were positioned as shields protecting Joel's 16th spot in the tournament rankings.

This meant that players who started the round far back in the overall standings had suddenly passed 13 players before they even hit a shot in round four. This created all kinds of scenarios and people who had been mathematically eliminated from contention were back in the mix.

Suddenly, Joel and others directly above him were very much at risk of being bumped out and the victory celebrations a week earlier seemed very much out of place now.

Joel didn't know quite what to do and was in a totally helpless position. So, he and Lona jumped in the car, headed for Napa and turned on the smart phone to follow the finish.

***

Lewiston, Idaho – Geno Bonnalie was hanging out with son Hudson when he first checked in and he was as shocked as Joel. He texted a friend to warn him and the friend went right to the Golf Channel to nervously watch the live action. Geno doesn't get the Golf Channel at home but he didn't want to watch anyway. He turned down an invitation to visit and watch. He couldn't keep his eyes off his cell phone though and was assessing every shot and scenario.

Could this really be happening? After the year of trials and episodes of great disappointment could they actually have the card yanked from them because of a rain storm and questionable administrative decision? It appeared so.

***

Atlantic Beach, Florida - This was especially true because playing companion in rounds one and two, Seamus Power had been the only threesome member to make the 36-hole cut. Now, with two par fives in front of him, it looked like he would displace Joel and claim the 25th and final playoff slot. All he needed was one birdie in the final three holes.

He didn't convert on the first opportunity, settling for par. Then he dumped a chip in a bunker and bogeyed the next hole. Still others could also pass both of them with strong finishes and a tense hour was playing out.

Luckily for Joel and Geno, other players couldn't muster a strong finish either and a couple actually fell backwards which allowed Joel to end in the 24th slot while Power edged in at the 25th and final safe position.

Still, the drop in rankings will very likely have negative implications pretty quickly. Joel is now very much on the bubble for getting in the Las Vegas and Mexico City fields which could lead to a slower than hoped for start to the 2017 – 2018 season. But for an hour or so, it looked much, much bleaker than that.

When all the smoke had cleared, five players had moved into the top 25 and five had been moved out.

Moving In and Securing PGA Card
Jonathan Byrd started 66th finished 2nd
Shawn Stefani 47th to 7th
Matt Jones 46th to 17th
Cameron Tringale 49th to 18th
Tom Hoge 31st to 20th

Moving Out
Adam Svenson 17th to 26th
Ben Crane 18th to 27th
Matthew Southgate 18th to 28th
Ryo Ishikawa 22nd to 31st
Cameron Percy 25th to 29th

This was indeed a double bad luck whammy for Southgate who had been the victim of the very strange leaf incident the week prior. Two flukes in two weeks had to be very hard to swallow.

***

WINNER'S CIRCLE – It was an amazing week for veteran Tiger Jonathan Byrd. He focused hard down the stretch and played away from trouble to protect his three-stroke lead. He closed with yet another birdie and finished with a truly impressive 24 under par for the tournament and was the only Tiger to earn his card.

What may have been even more impressive is how he turned his golf game around in one week. At the DAP, he had missed the cut with a disheartening nine over par effort.

The unhappy story of the rain out belonged to Ben Crane. He was one of the victims of the mass withdrawals who seemed in early in the week but ended up out of the final 25.

CHAPTER TEN
GOING FORWARD
TOOLS

Most athletes set annual goals for themselves as a future roadmap for improvement. Joel Dahmen is a bright, motivated guy who understands the value of this process and how planning can be valuable. It was the power of his mind that pulled him up when he was struggling late in the season.

Now, with a full year of PGA golf under his belt, he has a great understanding of what it will take to advance his position in the world of big league golf. He has seen the Tigers first-hand and lived with them. He even played with the biggest Tiger of them all and more than held his own.

He also knows that most top players do things differently than other people and many use tools to enhance their performance. These include hard, focused practice sessions, aggressive physical fitness regimes and sports psychology. Joel doesn't use any of these tools but is in a great position to decide if any or all of them would be right for him.

He may decide to simply keep doing the things that got him this far in the first place. They have obviously worked because he will still be walking with the Tigers next year and very few players ever rise to the level he has already attained in the world of golf.

Or, he may choose to change and do things somewhat differently moving forward. Three options for him to look at are:

FOCUSED PRACTICE – Joel certainly does practices and uses a swing coach and modern technology to help him improve. But Joel definitely spends less time working on his game than many of his peers and he does not have a disciplined schedule that includes a structured practice regime.

Part of this is because he tends to be almost perfect when he is on the practice tee hitting shots and he believes whacking a ton of balls doesn't accomplish much. His swing coach agrees and thinks tinkering with Joel's mechanics might not be positive.

However, most of the all-time greats of the game credit long practice hours as a key to their ultimate success and people like Jim Furyk, Jack Nicklaus, Tom Watson, Tiger Woods, Lee Trevino and Vijah Singh were known as practice fanatics.

Two quotes from the Pro Tour Golf College make a strong case. First, "The great ones never got to a stage where they thought that they have practiced enough and that they could cruise from that point forward. Second, "Truth is that it's not ability that stops most golfers from reaching a higher rung on the golf success ladder; it's the lack of drive to practice more than the majority."

Also, year-end statistics show that Joel has room for improvement especially around the greens. He finished the regular season far below average in vital short game rankings.

He was not listed in the year-end statistics because he didn't have a big enough sample size but three quarters of the way through the year he was -.245 in shots gained around the green which placed him 174th among his fellow PGA professionals. He was -.459 in putting which put him behind 180 of his peers and was 124th in total scrambling with a 57.72 par save percentage. In sand saves, he was unranked in the top 196 players listed which means he was somewhere below that.

**

PHYSICAL FITNESS- Developing a workout routine is another area Joel can consider for the future. Gary Player was the first big name professional to preach about the benefits of physical fitness and it's hard to deny he was very special when it came to being a picture of health and a symbol of golfing longevity. Then along came Tiger Woods who took fitness to a whole new level.

In recent years, the game's biggest Tigers have joined the fitness parade and are vocal advocates for the benefits associated with hard work out routines. These include Jim Furyk, Jason Day, Rory McIlroy, Billy Horschel, Rickie Fowler, Davis Love III, Martin Kaymer, Gary Woodland, KJ Choi, Camillo Villegas, Adam Scott, Matt Kucher, Zach Johnson and Dustin Johnson to name a few. Dustin Johnson says simply "Most of the guys at the top are all really hard-core into fitness and almost all do some kind of weight training on a regular basis."

In fact, workouts have become so important that at each PGA venue two large trailers are set up. One houses a mobile gym with weights, treadmills, elliptical machines, bikes, medicine balls and more. The other is a physical therapy center with therapists, nutritionists, chiropractors, treatment tables and electrical stimulation and ultrasound machines.

According to Jeff Hendra, one of three full-time therapists who staff the trailers, there is regular communications regarding golfer's specific needs. Several players including McIlroy arrive as early as 7am for 60 – 90 minute workouts or treatment sessions.

"I started out on Tour in 2002, and we used to see anywhere between 25 and 35 percent of any given field in the trailers in any given week," said Scott Riehl, a former full-time and now part-time strength and conditioning coach for the PGA Tour. "We're now looking at between 75 and 85 percent of the field coming through."

The players work hard to increase their stamina, strength, mobility, flexibility and stability. They also work to avoid getting tired late in the stages of a pressure-filled round and to prevent injury.

Of course, one size doesn't fit all says Angel Cabrera while smoking a cigarette. "I never workout," he smiled.

Then there is John Daly and former Masters champion Craig Stadler, nicknamed The Walrus and Spaniard Miguel Angel Jimenez who makes no secret of his love for wine, rich food and Cuban cigars. Even golf's most successful Tiger ever, Jack Nicklaus, was once called "fat Jack" when he first started winning tournaments.

Still, this might be worth a look on Joel's part. He is now thirty and it is never too early to think about longevity.

***

SPORTS PSYCHOLOGY – Veteran Golfer Kirk Triplett was once asked by a young man who wanted to get to the PGA for some tips of how to practice and how to achieve his goal. Kirk responded by sharing his own practice routine and introduced him to his sports psychologist.

Every year Triplett would take a rest and then start preparing for the coming year. This always included one-on-one time with his psychologist because Triplett felt getting mentally ready to play was more important than getting physically ready. His advice to the young man was to tackle the mental side of things very early in his career.

Triplett is certainly credible because he is a role model for the values of hard work and tenacity. He was nothing special during his high school years and was not recruited by any of the collegiate golf powerhouses. He ended up playing for the University of Nevada Reno and got his degree in 1985. At that point, he turned professional but his road to the PGA was not an easy one.

He paid his dues by playing in the Australian, Asian and Canadian tours before finally earning his PGA card in 1989. He won three PGA events and was a consistent contender who earned over $20,000,000 before losing his playing privileges in 2011. He joined the Champions Tour soon after and has been one of the top senior players ever since.

Some players have burst on the PGA scene right out of college and became instant stars but Triplett's rise is actually more typical of most players currently on the Tour. He wasn't born a golfer he made himself one.

***

Sports psychology is certainly nothing new. Athletes have been using specialists in this discipline for decades and there are numerous books on the subject. Joel Dahmen has done plenty of reading on the art of self-image psychology and is intellectually in tune with the message. However, he has not sought out one of the field's experts for individual consultation.

Many of the Tigers have used or are using this tool very effectively. Some have simply taken a class or paid for a few consultations while others have a psychologist on retainer and meet with them frequently.

Current and past stars listed as clients of the ten best known specialists reads like a list of golf royalty. Included are: Annika Sorenstam. Christie Kerr, Jason Day, Jason Dufner, Billy Hoerschel, Bernard Langer, Tom Watson, Zach Johnson, Lucas Glover, Ernie Els, Graeme McDowell, Keegan Bradley, Padraig Harrington, Darren Clark, Ray Floyd, Tom Kite, Nice Price, Justin Rose, Matt Kucher, Corey Pavin, Larry Mize, David Duval, Bo Van Pelt, Payne Stewart, Greg Norman, Nick Faldo and Ben Crenshaw.

Joel has joked that he should be called Ranger Rick because he is so solid on the practice tee. Could one of these specialists help him take his A game from the practice tee to the first tee of an important tournament? Certainly the option to give that a try is there for him.

CHAPTER ELEVEN
REFLECTIONS

The difficulty of making it to the PGA Tour is almost impossible to overstate. There are tens of thousands of talented players worldwide who have this as their ultimate goal. To achieve this is reserved for an elite few who have incredible God-given talent, a strong mind and a heavy dose of determination.

Joel Dahmen is one of the rare ones who actually made it to the mountain where the big Tigers live. The record of his year gives some solid credence to the point of view that staying there is almost as hard as getting there in the first place.

Now Joel and his faithful caddie and friend Geno Bonnalie will be coming back for their second year. They have fought through all of the rookie traps that await first year PGA players and, in their case, were compounded by getting fewer tournament starts than any other player with a card.

They had even survived a major curve ball on the final day of the Web.com playoffs.

History shows that the biggest and most established Tigers are going to breeze through next season with ease. The Dustin Johnsons, Jordan Spieths, Jason Days, Rory McIlroys and a few others will win tournaments, get endorsements galore, travel in private jets like royalty, make Ryder Cup teams and one day end up in the golf Hall-of-Fame.

Then there is the next layer of Tigers who will win plenty of money, continue to live very well and reap the benefits of being an established top fifty player.

The third level will consist of players who will play very well, make plenty of money, enjoy the glamorous lifestyle of the tour and have a comfortable

WALKING WITH TIGERS

year in all respects. They will not worry about getting their cards back for the next campaign.

The other 125 or so will still enjoy all of the wonderful upsides of the PGA Tour and most will do well financially. But, many will be back in the Web.com Tour playoffs next season because that is the nature of the highly competitive world of big league golf.

Where will Joel Dahmen be on this scale? Only time will tell but his odds of having a nice season are quite good. The experiences he had in his rookie season will likely serve him very well and his family and many friends have legitimate reason to be optimistic.

***

One thing is certain. Joel and Geno earned their right to fight another season. Nothing was handed to them.

The season had started with a series of missed cuts and lack of income that goes with that. This created low morale, self-doubt, financial worries and natural frustration. Then there was the disappointment of not getting in tournaments they had been counting on and had traditionally been available to all players in previous years.

Plus, things got worse before they got better. There were some tournaments like the one in Wilmington that made one question their ability to successfully compete at this level.

Life was not a bed of roses for player or caddie.

The great head-to-head dual with Dustin Johnson, the check that went with that and the great follow-up in Memphis seemed to turn around the season. Now, the worst was behind. The future looked great. Damn the torpedoes, full steam ahead!

Also, there was now a full schedule of events ahead. Nine weeks of play in a row – eight PGA events. Time to move up the FedEx list and cinch the card for the 2017 – 18 season! Big checks in the immediate future!

BEEP. WRONG. Didn't happen that way.

High points. Low points. Reflection and vow for more patience. Getting it together for the Web.Com Playoffs. Success. Earned back PGA playing privileges. Yahoo!

All of this was the forerunner of the rather strange scene in Cleveland where Geno put his arm around Joel's shoulders and the two looked happy despite the fact that Joel had just made a double bogey on the 18th hole. The irony of that kind of capsulized the season.

***

Comments following the cinching of coveted PGA card for next season:

JOEL DAHMEN – "The heat of keeping my card is now off and I'm really looking forward to next season. I've already made arrangements for a practice round with Nick and McKenzie for the Safeway (the season opener in Napa Valley, California). Knowing what to expect with the travel and golf courses is going to help me next year and I'm optimistic I will do well.

I agree the week off and my thoughts about patience were helpful. Also, I'm much more appreciative of what I have and of my place in life. I know I am a lucky to be able to what I do."

GENO BONNALIE – "I knew exactly where we were coming down the final stretch on Sunday and I was so glad to be walking off the green with our card intact for next year. I didn't give a hoot about the double. It meant nothing in terms of the big picture.

I love it out here and now I think we have a chance to do something special next year because of the experience we gained this go round. I have been nervous for several weeks. I had confidence all along that Joel would find a way to get it done in the playoffs but nothing is a sure thing in this game.

Plus, I don't think I would have come back for another season on the Web. The potential to make money for my family just isn't possible on the Web and I would have probably stayed in Lewiston and gone to work for my dad. In one way that would have been okay because I would be with Holly and Hudson but my heart and soul is golf and caddying for Joel is my dream job. I would have missed it terribly."

ROB RASHELL – "Lona was worried about next year and I told her hey, if the worst thing that happens to you is spending one more year on the Web Tour, life will be just fine because he IS going to make it. And, I truly believed and never doubted that for a minute. Joel has the talent and the mind to go very far in this game. I think he will have a great career.

I know going back to the Web would have been a downer. I get it. But really, Joel has done great in terms of a career path. He was the co-leader of a PGA event, played with the world's best player and had a top ten finish as a rookie. Plus, the nine week tournament stretch hardened him as experience can do. The only way to learn to manage adversary is to experience it.

He is light years better than he was a year ago. Think of this. Last year he choked at Pumpkin Ridge when the heat was on. He wasn't ready to handle that kind of pressure. This year, two things showed up. First, and probably under-appreciated, was the putt he made on number 18 at the Nationwide in the first playoff event which allowed him to make the cut. Second, we all saw how he played this weekend with the pressure on. He was great."

LONA SKUTT – "I was in Mexico on a family trip but we got the Golf Channel and I was glued to it on Sunday. I have said before how hard it is to watch someone you love play golf. You are happy when they do well but you feel so helpless when they don't because there is absolutely nothing you can do to help them.

It was a tough year with many lows. The worst was the Wilmington Tournament because Joel was SO incredibly down after getting beat up that bad. He was shook and I hurt for him. There were other lows too and I worried too much about credit card bills because I'm an old-fashioned worry wart.

But then we had the great, exciting finish in Dallas and things were better. But, he had a long way to go to get his card back. We never talked about that because neither Joel nor I wanted to address the potential negative. But, the worry was always there for me and in private moments, I thought about staying home and getting a job if he didn't get his PGA privileges back.

Now, I can relax a bit and enjoy my great life and my great guy."

HOLLY BONNALIE – Holly spend the morning of the final round in church and then went to Jim Bonnalie's man cave to watch the golf action unfold with Geno's parents, Jim and JoAnne. The night before Geno told her a top seven finish would put them in good position to get the card so she knew things were close down the stretch.

"I'm more at peace than relieved. I'm happy to know what next year's future will hold but I wasn't stressed out our anything because I know Geno,

Hudson and I are going to do okay no matter what. Not much keeps me awake at night.

Still, I am so happy for Geno. I can't imagine him not having golf in his life and, despite the hectic travel, he loves his job. Plus, I know he is a big asset to Joel. Geno is so positive he picks people up when they are down and Joel needs that. I think they are going to have a very good year.

Also, now that we know the scenario I can sit down with Geno and work out a schedule. Think I will go to five tournaments or so and Hudson is going to go on a couple of them. We'll see the country and have some fun," Holly said.

Holly didn't hesitate when asked about her highs and lows during the year. "Golf is such an emotional game and Geno was down in the dumps after one particular tournament in North Carolina. It's not like him to stay unhappy but seeing him the week after that trip made me hurt with him. That was the low.

The high? My sister's wedding was the same weekend as Joel's best finish of the year. Now that was great," Holly laughed.

BOB YOSAITIS – "I think of Joel as my own son and I was so happy after the Sunday night in Cleveland! I was worried. I know Joel wants to get married and buy a house. I also know he is a bit reluctant to take the step with uncertainty in his life. It would be fun to see him on a Ryder Cup team someday but more than that, I just want him to have a good and comfortable life. I'm really rooting for him to make a bunch of money next year and build a nest egg. I'm also hoping he will take the steps he needs to get better. Mostly, I'm proud of him."

ED DAHMEN – "He hasn't locked up a spot yet. I'm from Missouri, show me." (Ed proved to be the prophet on this) "But, I got to watch him a couple of times this year and I know he belongs. He can compete out here for sure and I'm very optimistic about his future. One thing I like is, if you look at Joel's record, he gets better as he gets comfortable.

In Canada, he didn't do worth beans the first year then got the Award of Merit in his second year. Same on the Web. He didn't do much as a rookie then got in the top 25. He will probably do better on the PGA the second time around too."

NICK TAYLOR – "He made it and I'm happy for him. He survived the toughest route imaginable when it came to keeping his card. Not only were his starts limited due to his qualifying position, but it was the toughest year ever for guys coming from the Web.com Tour. As an example, the year I earned my card I was in the 37th position and I got in every event. This year, the guy ranked 37th missed Mexico City and Las Vegas in the fall schedule. It was just that kind of year for the rookies. Starts were hard to come by and this put Joel way behind the eight ball from day one.

The grind of Monday qualifying and waiting until the last possible moment to see if you are actually going to get to play in a tournament grind on a guy and create extra distractions and stress that makes a hard job even harder. It is still hard, but he endured the worst possible scenario.

I know he can play out here. He has proven that. I think he is going to have a good year."

CHAPTER TWELVE
HAPPY TRAILS

Joel Dahmen and Geno Bonnalie are good guys and it is no surprise they have loving and very special women in their lives. Lona and Holly are warm and extremely supportive people who understand what it takes for their guys to walk with the Tigers.

Ironically, the guys who had traveled together and been through bed bugs, fire ants, the freezing winds of Pebble Beach, the sweltering heat of Auburn, Alabama, the bitter disappointment of North Carolina, the pure joy of Dallas, the nagging fear of failure, the super high of success and finally, the one last scare in Florida, would be starting their new season traveling separate roads.

Joel was in the PGA field at Napa, California and Geno made a decision to be there as his caddie. Joel overruled him.

In September, Geno had qualified to play in the prestigious Mid-Amateur Tournament finals in Atlanta. Geno decided to skip that and attend the Napa PGA opener but Joel put his foot down. "I'll be fine with a substitute. You have qualified for a USGA event and you need to be there," Dahmen said firmly.

Geno protested mildly but knew his friend was right. "The Mid-Am really is a pretty big deal and though I'm probably not good enough to win, I do owe it to myself to compete and see what I can do," Geno admitted.

So the new season, full of promise, kicked off with Joel in the wine country of Northern California and Geno on a jet en route to the metropolitan Southeast. But, the separation would be short-lived. The new PGA road lies dead ahead.

Happy trails, dear friends.

View other Black Rose Writing titles at www.blackrosewriting.com/books and use promo code **PRINT** to receive a **20% discount** when purchasing.

BLACK ROSE writing™